Love in 2025
A Modern Valentine's Tale

Introduction

In the year 2025, love is no longer confined to handwritten letters or fleeting glances across crowded rooms. It has transcended time and space, woven intricately into the very fabric of our digital lives. The advent of cutting-edge technology has revolutionized the way we connect, date, and fall in love. From swiping right on apps powered by artificial intelligence to sharing heartfelt moments in the immersive worlds of the metaverse, the quest for love in this modern era is as thrilling as it is complex. Yet, despite the innovations, the essence of love—its vulnerability, its beauty, and its challenges—remains timeless.

This book delves into the kaleidoscope of love in 2025, exploring how technology has redefined relationships without erasing their emotional core. We journey through stories of digital connections that blossom into real-world romance, the rise of AI companions as emotional partners, and the unexpected ways technology both simplifies and complicates modern love. Along the way, we confront questions that linger in the shadows of progress: Can an algorithm truly predict compatibility? How do we maintain authenticity in a world of curated profiles and augmented realities? And most importantly, where does the human heart fit in a future so dominated by machines?

Through heartfelt narratives, expert insights, and thought-provoking discussions, Love in 2025 invites you to reflect on the evolving dynamics of romance in this extraordinary age. Whether you are a hopeless romantic navigating virtual dating or a skeptic wary of love's digital evolution, this book offers a lens to understand

and embrace the ever-changing landscape of relationships. At its core, it is a celebration of love's resilience and adaptability—proof that no matter the era, love continues to find a way.

Chapter 1
The Digital Cupid

In 2025, love is no longer left to chance meetings or serendipitous encounters. Instead, algorithms play the role of modern-day matchmakers, meticulously sifting through data points to create what they claim are perfect matches. These "digital cupids" operate behind the screens of dating apps and platforms, using advanced machine learning and artificial intelligence to decode compatibility. They promise to take the guesswork out of love, replacing awkward introductions with curated connections based on shared interests, values, and even genetic compatibility. But as we entrust matters of the heart to technology, one must ask: Are these algorithms truly guiding us toward love, or merely simulating its surface?

The allure of digital matchmaking lies in its precision and efficiency. A single swipe can open the door to potential partners from across the globe, offering possibilities that were unimaginable just a few decades ago. Yet, for all its convenience, the rise of algorithmic romance raises profound questions about the nature of love itself. Can compatibility be reduced to data points? How do we account for the unpredictable spark of chemistry or the serendipity of shared experiences? The role of the digital cupid, while groundbreaking, is not without its limitations. It often overlooks the complexities and nuances of human connection, favoring patterns and predictability over the raw, messy beauty of falling in love.

This chapter explores the fascinating world of algorithmic romance, unraveling the promises and pitfalls of digital matchmaking. Through real-life stories and expert perspectives, we delve into how these technologies are shaping relationships in ways both profound and unexpected. As we navigate this new terrain, we are reminded that while digital cupids can set the stage, the performance of love remains a deeply human art, requiring vulnerability, effort, and the courage to embrace the unknown.

Love in the Age of Algorithms

The concept of love has always been rooted in mystery and unpredictability, a dance of serendipity and chance that brought two souls together. In the digital age, however, love has taken a sharp turn into the realm of data, with algorithms now playing the role of matchmaker. These complex computational systems analyze a plethora of data points—from personal preferences and shared interests to personality traits and even online behavior—to determine compatibility. This new era of algorithmic matchmaking is reshaping how we think about love, promising efficiency and precision in the quest to find a partner.

At its core, algorithmic love hinges on the belief that compatibility can be quantified. Dating apps and platforms employ sophisticated machine learning models to analyze profiles and behavior, using this information to suggest matches that align with a user's desires and lifestyle. For instance, some platforms prioritize shared interests, while others delve deeper, analyzing values, communication styles, and long-term goals. The promise is compelling: no more blind dates, awkward small talk, or wasted time. Instead, these platforms offer curated connections that cater to specific needs, from casual dating to serious relationships.

However, this reliance on algorithms also raises significant questions. Can love truly be distilled into a series of data points?

Human connections are inherently complex, often driven by intangibles like chemistry, intuition, and shared experiences. Algorithms excel at identifying patterns but often fail to capture the nuances of human emotion and attraction. For example, they might overlook the importance of a fleeting glance, an unplanned moment of vulnerability, or the indescribable pull of shared laughter. By focusing on measurable traits, these systems risk oversimplifying love, reducing it to a transaction rather than a profound, transformative experience.

Moreover, the efficiency of algorithms can sometimes lead to unexpected challenges. The paradox of choice—where an abundance of options makes it harder to commit—becomes particularly pronounced in the world of online dating. Users often find themselves swiping endlessly, unsure if the next profile might be "better" than the last. This creates a culture of disposability, where potential matches are discarded for minor flaws or superficial reasons. The ease of digital connections can also lead to superficial interactions, with users treating relationships as fleeting rather than meaningful.

Yet, it's undeniable that algorithms have also brought significant benefits to modern love. They have made dating more accessible, particularly for those in marginalized communities or with unconventional preferences. They allow people to connect across vast distances, fostering global relationships that transcend traditional boundaries. For many, these platforms serve as a lifeline, offering the chance to meet partners they might never have encountered in their daily lives.

As we embrace this new era of love, it's crucial to strike a balance between technology and humanity. Algorithms can provide a starting point, a way to filter possibilities and open doors. But the essence of love—the vulnerability, the effort, and the willingness to grow together—remains deeply human. Love in the age of algorithms is not about replacing serendipity but enhancing it, using technology as a tool to navigate the ever-changing landscape of relationships while holding onto the timeless truths of connection and intimacy.

Swiping for Soulmates

The act of finding a soulmate has undergone a dramatic transformation with the rise of dating apps and platforms, where a simple swipe has become the gateway to potential love stories. What once required chance encounters or carefully orchestrated introductions is now facilitated by a flick of the thumb. The concept of "swiping for soulmates" reflects the modern era of dating, where technology mediates human connection and provides unprecedented access to a vast pool of potential partners. This shift has not only redefined how people meet but also reshaped the expectations and experiences of romance.

At its heart, the swiping mechanism is deceptively simple. Users are presented with profiles featuring photos, brief bios, and often a list of interests or shared values. A swipe to the right indicates interest, while a swipe to the left signifies disinterest. When two users swipe right on each other, it's a match—a moment filled with potential. This gamification of dating is a masterstroke of design, combining instant gratification with the promise of meaningful connections. It taps into human psychology, offering a sense of accomplishment and validation with every match.

However, the simplicity of swiping masks the complexity and emotional weight behind the process. For many, the ease of rejecting or accepting profiles fosters a superficial approach to dating, where appearances and quick judgments take precedence over deeper qualities. The paradox of choice becomes apparent as users swipe through endless options, often questioning if the perfect match might be just one more swipe away. This abundance can lead to indecision and a tendency to view potential partners as disposable, undermining the depth and commitment required to build lasting relationships.

The dynamics of swiping also bring unique challenges to those seeking soulmates. Algorithms designed to prioritize compatibility often struggle with intangible factors like chemistry or shared experiences. While a profile might check all the boxes on paper, real-world interactions can reveal unexpected incompatibilities. Conversely, people who might not initially seem like a perfect match could surprise each other with a connection that grows over time. The reliance on digital profiles can unintentionally filter out these serendipitous discoveries.

Yet, for all its flaws, swiping has undeniably democratized the dating landscape. It offers opportunities for people who might struggle to meet potential partners through traditional means, whether due to busy schedules, geographical constraints, or personal preferences. Many users have found genuine, enduring love through these platforms, proving that meaningful connections can emerge even in a system designed for speed and efficiency. Stories of couples who met through swiping highlight the adaptability of human relationships and the enduring power of love.

To navigate the world of swiping successfully, it's essential to approach it with intention and balance. While the swipe-right culture encourages quick decisions, taking the time to engage meaningfully with matches can foster deeper connections. Being authentic in creating profiles and engaging in conversations helps ensure that the virtual interaction translates into real-world compatibility. Ultimately, swiping for soulmates is not about finding perfection but about being open to the possibilities that technology offers, while staying grounded in the timeless truths of love and connection.

The Promise of Perfect Matches

In a world driven by data and algorithms, the idea of finding a "perfect match" has become a tantalizing prospect. Gone are the days of relying solely on chance meetings or the matchmaking efforts of friends and family. Today, dating platforms promise to leverage the power of artificial intelligence and machine learning to deliver curated matches that align with our deepest desires and preferences. This promise of perfect matches speaks to the human yearning for connection, while simultaneously revealing the intricate interplay between technology and emotion in the quest for love.

The allure of perfect matches lies in their precision. Dating platforms collect vast amounts of user data, including personality traits, lifestyle preferences, communication styles, and even values. By analyzing this information, they aim to identify compatibility patterns that might otherwise go unnoticed. These platforms use complex algorithms to suggest potential partners, often claiming to predict long-term relationship success based on factors like shared interests, emotional compatibility, and life goals. For those navigating the often-daunting world of modern dating, this scientific approach offers hope and efficiency—a way to cut through the noise and focus on meaningful connections.

Yet, the idea of a "perfect match" is inherently subjective, shaped by individual expectations and cultural influences. While algorithms excel at identifying shared traits, they struggle to account for the ineffable elements of love—chemistry, timing, and the unpredictable dynamics that arise in real-world interactions. What seems perfect on paper may not translate to a fulfilling relationship. Conversely, some of the most profound connections defy algorithmic logic, emerging from unexpected places or with partners who initially appear to be mismatched.

Another challenge lies in the pressure created by the promise of perfection. When presented with a match labeled as "highly compatible," individuals may approach the connection with heightened expectations, scrutinizing every interaction for signs of alignment. This can lead to disappointment if the reality falls short of the ideal, or it may even prevent people from fully embracing the natural growth and imperfections inherent in any relationship. The quest for perfection risks overshadowing the joy of discovering and nurturing love in its raw, unfiltered form.

Despite these complexities, the promise of perfect matches has undeniable benefits. For many, these platforms have provided access to potential partners who might otherwise remain out of reach. They have empowered individuals to take control of their romantic lives, offering tools and insights that were once unavailable. Moreover, the data-driven approach can help users gain a deeper understanding of their own preferences and needs, fostering greater self-awareness in the process.

Ultimately, the promise of perfect matches is less about guaranteeing love and more about creating opportunities. Algorithms can open doors and provide starting points, but the essence of connection—vulnerability, effort, and shared experiences—remains deeply human. In embracing this technology, it is important to balance optimism with realism, recognizing that while perfection may be an illusion, the journey toward meaningful relationships is a profoundly rewarding endeavor. The true beauty of love lies not in its precision but in its capacity to surprise, inspire, and transform.

Chapter 2
Virtual Heartbeats

In the digital age, the sound of a heartbeat is no longer confined to physical proximity. Love now pulses through screens and devices, forming connections that transcend time zones and geographical boundaries. Virtual relationships have become a defining feature of modern romance, with couples building deep emotional bonds through text messages, video calls, and shared virtual experiences. While the absence of physical touch once seemed like an insurmountable barrier, technology has redefined intimacy, allowing people to forge meaningful connections in entirely new ways.

The rise of virtual relationships reflects both the opportunities and challenges of modern connectivity. On one hand, technology has brought people closer, enabling couples to stay connected despite physical distance. Digital tools like video calls and shared online activities provide a sense of presence, allowing couples to communicate and share their lives in ways that were unimaginable a few decades ago. On the other hand, the reliance on virtual interactions introduces unique complexities. Miscommunication can easily arise when nonverbal cues are absent, and maintaining emotional intimacy requires intentional effort and creativity.

Yet, virtual relationships also highlight the resilience and adaptability of love. Whether it's navigating long-distance relationships or meeting a partner entirely online, couples are finding innovative ways to bridge the gap between the virtual and the real.

Virtual heartbeats are more than a testament to technological advancement; they are a reminder that love, in all its forms, is capable of evolving and flourishing in the most unexpected circumstances. This chapter explores the nuances of virtual connections, offering insights into how technology is shaping the way we experience, express, and sustain love in a digital world.

Building Connections in Cyberspace

In a world increasingly defined by digital interactions, building meaningful connections in cyberspace has become an art form. Technology has opened doors to a vast universe of possibilities, allowing people to connect across time zones, cultures, and experiences. For millions, cyberspace has evolved from a tool of convenience to a cornerstone of modern relationships. While some question the authenticity of digital connections, others embrace the profound impact that virtual interactions can have on fostering real emotional bonds.

The journey of building connections online often begins with shared platforms. Social media, forums, dating apps, and even multiplayer games provide spaces where individuals can engage with others who share their interests, values, or aspirations. These digital spaces allow people to bypass the limitations of geography and expand their social circles in unprecedented ways. Whether it's forming a deep friendship in an online community or meeting a romantic partner through a dating app, cyberspace creates opportunities for connections that might never occur in the physical world.

One of the greatest strengths of building connections in cyberspace is its ability to foster emotional intimacy through communication. In virtual interactions, people often feel freer to express their thoughts and feelings, unhindered by the pressures of face-to-face interactions. Text messaging, video calls, and voice chats provide tools for sharing life's joys and challenges, helping individuals form deep emotional bonds. For some, the act of writing out their thoughts allows for greater self-expression, making online conversations a fertile ground for genuine connections.

However, the process of building connections in cyberspace is not without its challenges. The lack of physical presence can make it harder to interpret nonverbal cues like tone, facial expressions, and body language, which are essential for understanding context and emotion. Miscommunication can occur when messages are read differently than intended, leading to potential misunderstandings. Furthermore, the anonymity and distance provided by the digital world can sometimes create opportunities for deceit or misrepresentation, as people may choose to present curated or exaggerated versions of themselves.

Despite these hurdles, many connections built in cyberspace transition successfully into the physical world. Virtual interactions often serve as a starting point, providing a foundation of trust and familiarity before meeting in person. For couples navigating long-distance relationships, technology becomes an invaluable tool for maintaining closeness, with video calls, shared online activities, and virtual dates serving as lifelines. Even for friendships and professional connections, the ability to connect online provides opportunities to collaborate, share, and grow together.

Ultimately, building connections in cyberspace requires intentionality and authenticity. By approaching digital relationships with honesty and care, individuals can form bonds that are as meaningful and enduring as those formed in person. Cyberspace is not a substitute for real-world interactions, but a powerful extension of them—a bridge that connects hearts and minds across the vastness of the digital landscape. In embracing the opportunities of this new frontier, we discover that the essence of connection remains the same, regardless of the medium: the desire to be seen, understood, and valued.

The Role of AI in Modern Relationships

Artificial Intelligence (AI) has permeated nearly every aspect of human life, and relationships are no exception. From matchmaking algorithms on dating apps to virtual assistants offering advice on relationship conflicts, AI is reshaping how people connect, communicate, and maintain their bonds. Its role in modern relationships extends beyond convenience, acting as both a tool and a catalyst for navigating the complexities of human emotions. As AI continues to evolve, it challenges traditional notions of intimacy, compatibility, and even love itself.

One of the most significant contributions of AI to relationships is its ability to facilitate connections. Dating platforms like Tinder, Bumble, and eHarmony use advanced algorithms to analyze user data and predict compatibility. These systems consider factors such as shared interests, personality traits, and lifestyle preferences to suggest potential matches. By narrowing the search for a partner, AI simplifies the dating process, allowing individuals to focus on building connections rather than searching for them. This targeted approach has transformed how people meet, making relationships more accessible in a fast-paced, digitally driven world.

Beyond matchmaking, AI has also become a mediator in relationships. Virtual assistants like Siri, Alexa, and Google Assistant now offer reminders for anniversaries, suggest date ideas, or even play calming music during conflicts. AI-powered tools like Replika and Woebot provide emotional support, helping users process feelings and improve communication skills. These technologies act as companions and coaches, guiding individuals through the challenges of modern relationships. For long-distance couples, AI-driven apps facilitate virtual dates, shared activities, and even real-time translations, bridging the physical gap with innovative solutions.

However, the growing reliance on AI in relationships raises important ethical and emotional questions. For instance, can AI truly understand human emotions, or is it merely simulating empathy? While AI can process language and analyze sentiment, it lacks the genuine emotional depth that defines human connections. This limitation becomes particularly significant in the context of AI companions—robots or chatbots designed to fulfill emotional needs. While these AI entities may provide comfort and companionship, they cannot replicate the complexity and authenticity of human relationships.

Another concern is the potential for AI to distort human interactions. The convenience of AI can sometimes lead to dependency, with individuals turning to technology for validation or conflict resolution rather than engaging with their partners directly. Additionally, the use of AI in monitoring relationships—such as tracking text messages or analyzing social media behavior—raises privacy issues and can erode trust. These dynamics highlight the need for careful consideration of AI's role in fostering, rather than hindering, healthy relationships.

Despite these challenges, AI holds immense promise for enhancing relationships when used thoughtfully. It can provide insights into behavior patterns, suggest strategies for improving communication, and even foster empathy by analyzing diverse perspectives. By acting as a facilitator rather than a replacement, AI can empower individuals to navigate the complexities of modern love with greater awareness and intentionality.

In the end, the role of AI in modern relationships is best viewed as a partnership. It is a tool to complement human connection, offering support and innovation while leaving the emotional heart of relationships intact. As we continue to integrate AI into our lives, the key will be to use it not to replace human intimacy but to deepen and enrich it, ensuring that love remains as vibrant and authentic as ever.

When Virtual Meets Reality

The line between virtual and real-world relationships has become increasingly blurred as technology advances. What begins as a connection through screens often transitions into real-life interactions, merging the digital and physical aspects of love. This intersection of virtual and reality has created new dynamics in modern relationships, redefining how people meet, communicate, and sustain emotional bonds. While it brings unprecedented opportunities for connection, it also introduces unique challenges that require adaptation and understanding.

For many, virtual platforms are the first step in forming a connection. Dating apps, social media, and online communities provide spaces where individuals can meet and get to know each other. These digital interactions often serve as a filter, allowing people to establish compatibility and mutual interest before investing in face-to-face meetings. This initial phase can be particularly appealing to those who are introverted, busy, or geographically distant from potential partners. The ability to interact in a low-pressure environment fosters openness and emotional intimacy, setting the stage for deeper connections.

However, when virtual relationships transition to reality, they face a new set of tests. The absence of nonverbal cues in virtual interactions, such as body language and tone of voice, can create discrepancies between how a person is perceived online and in person. While video calls and voice chats bridge some of this gap, they cannot fully replicate the complexities of in-person communication. Meeting in reality often brings surprises—both pleasant and challenging—as individuals adjust to each other's real-world presence, habits, and mannerisms.

The shift from virtual to reality also introduces logistical and emotional considerations. For couples in long-distance relationships, the transition may involve significant planning, travel, and even life changes. The anticipation of meeting in person can be both exciting and nerve-wracking, as it represents a pivotal moment in the relationship. Emotional stakes are heightened, with the potential for both deepening the bond or discovering incompatibilities that were not evident in the virtual realm. Navigating these transitions requires open communication, patience, and a willingness to adapt.

Despite the challenges, the meeting of virtual and reality often strengthens relationships. For many, the act of bridging the digital and physical worlds reinforces commitment and trust. Couples who successfully transition from virtual to real often report a deeper appreciation for each other, as they navigate the complexities of merging their lives. Shared experiences, such as traveling to meet or integrating into each other's social circles, become milestones that solidify the bond.

When virtual meets reality, it highlights the adaptability of human connection. While technology facilitates the initial stages of a relationship, the real-world interactions bring authenticity and depth. The key to a successful transition lies in balancing the convenience and accessibility of virtual connections with the irreplaceable richness of face-to-face encounters. By embracing both worlds, individuals can create relationships that are not only rooted in modern technology but also grounded in the timeless principles of love, understanding, and shared growth. This fusion of virtual and reality exemplifies how love continues to evolve while remaining profoundly human at its core.

Chapter 3
Love Beyond Borders

In an increasingly interconnected world, love knows no boundaries. The digital age has shattered geographical barriers, enabling people from diverse cultures and distant lands to connect, communicate, and fall in love. What once seemed improbable—romantic relationships spanning continents—is now a common reality, fueled by social media, dating apps, and video communication platforms. Love beyond borders has become a testament to the transformative power of technology, as it brings people together across vast physical and cultural divides.

While the allure of cross-border romance is undeniable, it also brings unique challenges. Language differences, cultural nuances, and the logistics of long-distance relationships can test even the strongest of connections. Couples navigating these relationships must embrace adaptability, empathy, and a willingness to bridge cultural gaps. At the same time, these challenges often lead to personal growth and a deeper understanding of the world, as individuals learn to appreciate perspectives beyond their own.

This chapter delves into the phenomenon of love beyond borders, exploring its joys and complexities. From stories of couples who overcame great distances to be together, to insights into how technology supports these relationships, it celebrates the resilience and adaptability of love in a globalized era. It is a reminder that while love may face obstacles, its ability to connect hearts across borders remains a timeless and universal force.

Erasing Distances with Technology

The evolution of technology has fundamentally transformed the way we connect with one another, making it possible to bridge even the most daunting physical distances. For those in long-distance relationships or international romances, technology serves as both a lifeline and a foundation for maintaining emotional intimacy. What was once a significant barrier to connection has now become an opportunity to build stronger relationships, thanks to tools that enable constant communication, shared experiences, and virtual proximity.

One of the most significant ways technology erases distance is through instant communication. Video calls via platforms like Zoom, FaceTime, and WhatsApp allow couples to see and hear each other in real-time, recreating the experience of being together. These interactions provide a level of intimacy that letters and phone calls of the past could never achieve, enabling partners to share their lives in vivid detail. Text messaging and voice notes also offer a continuous thread of connection throughout the day, ensuring that no moment feels too far apart.

Beyond communication, technology has introduced innovative ways for couples to share experiences, even when they are miles apart. Virtual reality (VR) platforms enable partners to explore digital worlds together, from taking a virtual stroll through a park to attending concerts and events. Streaming services like Netflix Party or Disney+ GroupWatch allow couples to watch movies and shows simultaneously, creating a shared sense of presence. Even multiplayer video games provide opportunities for collaboration and fun, fostering teamwork and deepening bonds. These shared experiences help couples maintain a sense of normalcy, even when separated by vast distances.

Social media also plays a critical role in bridging the gap. Platforms like Instagram, Facebook, and Snapchat allow couples to share snapshots of their daily lives, keeping each other updated on even the smallest details. These platforms act as windows into each other's worlds, helping partners feel more connected and involved despite the miles between them. Social media also provides opportunities to celebrate milestones, share memories, and express love publicly, reinforcing the relationship in meaningful ways.

However, technology is not without its challenges. The constant availability of digital communication can sometimes lead to overdependence or unrealistic expectations. Miscommunication is also a risk, as tone and context can be lost in text or digital interactions. Furthermore, the lack of physical touch—a cornerstone of human intimacy—can leave a gap that even the most advanced technology cannot fully bridge. Navigating these challenges requires open communication, trust, and an understanding of each partner's needs.

Despite these hurdles, technology has made love beyond borders more accessible and sustainable than ever before. It has allowed couples to defy geographical constraints, nurturing relationships that might otherwise have been impossible. As technology continues to evolve, it offers new ways to deepen connection and foster intimacy, ensuring that physical distance is no longer an insurmountable obstacle to love.

Ultimately, the power of technology lies not just in its ability to connect, but in its capacity to support and sustain the bonds that matter most. By erasing distances, it enables love to flourish in ways that are both innovative and timeless, proving that connection is not about proximity, but about the effort and intention we bring to our relationships.

Navigating Cultural Differences in the Digital World

The digital age has made it easier than ever to connect with people from different cultures and backgrounds. For relationships that span across countries, cultural diversity enriches the bond, offering opportunities to learn, grow, and appreciate new perspectives. However, it also presents unique challenges that require sensitivity, open-mindedness, and effort to overcome. Navigating cultural differences in the digital world is a nuanced journey that combines the excitement of cross-cultural exchange with the intricacies of understanding and adapting to one another's traditions and beliefs.

One of the most prominent aspects of navigating cultural differences in the digital space is communication. Language barriers can pose significant challenges, especially when subtle nuances and idiomatic expressions don't translate easily. However, technology provides tools to bridge this gap. Translation apps, multilingual keyboards, and real-time language translation services enable couples to communicate effectively, even if they don't share a common first language. Yet, successful communication goes beyond words—it requires empathy and a willingness to understand the context and meaning behind each message.

Cultural norms and values also play a critical role in shaping how people interact online. In some cultures, directness in communication is valued, while in others, subtlety and indirect expressions are preferred. Similarly, the use of emojis, tone, and humor may be interpreted differently across cultures. For instance, what might be seen as playful in one culture could come across as disrespectful in another. Being mindful of these differences helps foster mutual respect and prevents misunderstandings, laying a strong foundation for the relationship.

The digital world also allows for the exchange of cultural traditions and practices. Virtual celebrations of holidays, sharing recipes through video calls, or learning traditional dances via online platforms are ways for couples to engage with each other's heritage. Social media provides a window into cultural lifestyles, helping partners understand daily routines, family dynamics, and societal expectations. This exposure not only strengthens the relationship but also broadens one's worldview, encouraging personal growth and cultural appreciation.

However, cultural differences can sometimes lead to conflict, especially when values or expectations clash. For example, differing attitudes toward gender roles, family involvement, or personal independence can create friction. In these situations, it is crucial to address concerns with patience and openness, focusing on finding common ground rather than imposing one's own beliefs. Digital platforms enable couples to have these conversations in real-time, using tools like video calls or collaborative apps to work through challenges together.

Technology also plays a role in managing external perceptions of cross-cultural relationships. Families and communities may hold preconceived notions about certain cultures, and couples often find themselves bridging not just their own differences but also those of their broader social circles. Sharing stories, videos, or cultural experiences through digital platforms can help demystify stereotypes and foster acceptance.

Navigating cultural differences in the digital world is ultimately about embracing diversity while building a shared understanding. It requires curiosity, adaptability, and a commitment to growth. By leveraging technology to explore and celebrate each other's cultures, couples can create relationships that are enriched by their differences, proving that love transcends boundaries in the most meaningful ways.

The Challenges of a Global Love Affair

Falling in love across borders is an exhilarating journey, filled with the promise of cultural enrichment and personal growth. However, a global love affair also comes with its fair share of challenges, as couples navigate logistical, emotional, and societal complexities. These obstacles, while daunting, can become opportunities for growth and deeper connection if approached with patience and mutual understanding.

One of the most pressing challenges in global relationships is managing physical distance. Unlike local relationships, where couples can meet frequently, those separated by borders must contend with limited in-person interactions. Long stretches apart can lead to feelings of loneliness and insecurity, as physical presence plays a crucial role in fostering intimacy. Even with advancements in technology—video calls, instant messaging, and virtual dates—the inability to share daily, mundane moments together can create a sense of disconnection.

Time zones further complicate communication in global relationships. Scheduling calls or virtual dates requires careful planning, often leading to sacrifices in personal schedules. One partner might stay up late while the other wakes up early to make time for each other. While this effort demonstrates commitment, it can also lead to fatigue and stress over time. The lack of spontaneity in conversations and the constant reliance on scheduling can make the relationship feel like a logistical puzzle rather than a natural connection.

Cultural differences add another layer of complexity to global love affairs. While these differences can be enriching, they also bring potential for misunderstandings and conflicts. Variations in communication styles, family expectations, or societal norms can lead to friction. For instance, one partner may come from a culture that prioritizes individualism, while the other may value collective family decision-making. Navigating these disparities requires patience, compromise, and a willingness to learn from each other's perspectives.

Another significant challenge is the financial strain often associated with global relationships. Travel expenses, visa applications, and other logistical costs can add up quickly. For many couples, visiting each other requires careful budgeting and sacrifices in other areas of life. Additionally, the uncertainty of international travel restrictions, particularly in recent years, has made these visits even more unpredictable and stressful.

Societal perceptions and external pressures can also weigh heavily on global couples. Families and communities may harbor biases or prejudices about certain cultures, leading to judgment or lack of acceptance. Couples often find themselves not only bridging their own cultural differences but also educating their families and communities to foster understanding. The emotional toll of managing these external factors can be significant, requiring resilience and a united front.

Despite these challenges, many global couples find ways to thrive. They learn to communicate effectively, build trust over distance, and create shared rituals that strengthen their bond. The difficulties they face often deepen their appreciation for each other and reinforce their commitment to making the relationship work. Global love affairs, though challenging, are a testament to the resilience and adaptability of love in the modern era.

Ultimately, a global love affair is a journey of perseverance and growth. While the challenges are real, so too are the rewards of building a relationship that transcends borders. With effort, understanding, and the support of technology, couples can turn these obstacles into stepping stones toward a deeper and more meaningful connection.

Chapter 4
The Language of Love: Emojis and Beyond

In a world dominated by digital communication, the way we express love has evolved significantly. Emojis, GIFs, and memes have become the modern vocabulary of affection, adding visual and emotional depth to our messages. A simple heart emoji or a playful GIF can convey feelings that might otherwise be difficult to put into words. This digital shorthand has transformed how we connect emotionally, enabling us to express love across languages, cultures, and distances with a universal visual language.

While emojis and other digital expressions make communication more dynamic, they also come with their own set of challenges. The nuances of meaning can vary greatly depending on context and individual interpretation. For instance, a winking face might be seen as flirtatious to one person but playful to another. These subtle differences highlight the importance of understanding the recipient's perspective and the context of the interaction. The digital language of love, while innovative, requires careful navigation to avoid misunderstandings.

This chapter explores the evolution of love's digital lexicon, delving into how emojis and other tools have shaped modern relationships. From their ability to bridge communication gaps to the complexities they introduce, we examine how these visual cues enrich emotional expression in the digital age. At the heart of it all, the language of love—whether spoken, written, or visual—remains a powerful force that transcends platforms and continues to bring people closer together.

How Communication Has Evolved

The way we communicate has undergone a profound transformation over the years, influenced by advances in technology, shifts in social norms, and the globalization of cultures. From handwritten letters to instant messages, the evolution of communication reflects humanity's desire to connect more quickly, efficiently, and creatively. This transformation has reshaped relationships, including romantic ones, making it easier than ever to share emotions, build intimacy, and bridge distances. However, it has also introduced complexities that require us to adapt and navigate new dynamics.

In the past, communication in relationships was often slow and deliberate. Love letters, for instance, were carefully crafted and carried the weight of anticipation. These letters were a reflection of deep thought and emotional investment, allowing individuals to articulate their feelings in a timeless and meaningful way. While this form of communication fostered patience and a sense of permanence, it was limited by its inability to facilitate immediate interaction.

The invention of the telephone marked a turning point, enabling real-time voice conversations that brought immediacy and intimacy to relationships. Partners could hear each other's voices, share their thoughts instantly, and resolve misunderstandings in the moment. This technological leap bridged emotional gaps and laid the groundwork for the rapid advancements that followed.

The digital revolution of the late 20th and early 21st centuries introduced a new era of communication, with text messaging, emails, and social media becoming the norm. Platforms like Facebook, Instagram, and WhatsApp transformed how people interacted, allowing for constant connectivity. Emojis, GIFs, and memes emerged as tools for expressing emotions visually, adding layers of nuance to digital conversations. A simple smiley face could convey warmth, while a heart emoji could signify love, transcending linguistic barriers and creating a universal language.

As technology advanced further, video calls and virtual reality introduced new dimensions to communication. Couples could now see each other in real-time, regardless of geographical distance, making long-distance relationships more sustainable. Virtual reality platforms allowed partners to share immersive experiences, from watching a movie together to exploring virtual worlds. These innovations brought a sense of physical presence to digital interactions, blurring the lines between the virtual and real worlds.

Despite these advancements, the evolution of communication has also brought challenges. The immediacy of digital tools can sometimes lead to overcommunication or miscommunication, as tone and context are easily misunderstood in text-based interactions. The constant availability of messaging can create pressure to respond quickly, potentially leading to misunderstandings if expectations are not aligned. Additionally, the reliance on emojis and shorthand expressions, while efficient, can sometimes oversimplify complex emotions.

However, the evolution of communication is ultimately a story of adaptability and creativity. As tools and platforms change, people continue to find new ways to express themselves and deepen their connections. The essence of communication—understanding, empathy, and the desire to connect—remains unchanged, even as the methods evolve. By embracing the benefits of modern tools while being mindful of their limitations, individuals can navigate this dynamic landscape and foster meaningful relationships in an ever-changing world.

Misinterpretations in Text and Tone

In an era where digital communication dominates, one of the most common challenges in relationships is the misinterpretation of text and tone. While texting, emails, and messaging apps offer unparalleled convenience and immediacy, they often lack the subtle nuances of face-to-face or voice interactions. Without visual cues like facial expressions or auditory signals like intonation, written messages can be easily misconstrued, leading to confusion, frustration, or even conflict.

Text messages are inherently limited by their simplicity. A short message, meant to be casual or neutral, can come across as curt or dismissive to the recipient. For instance, a simple "Okay" might seem agreeable to the sender but appear passive-aggressive to the reader, depending on their mood or context. Similarly, humor, sarcasm, or irony often fall flat in text form. Without the cues that help clarify intent, these elements can be misinterpreted, causing unnecessary tension or misunderstanding between partners.

Emojis and punctuation were introduced to help bridge this gap, adding visual context to digital communication. A smiley face can soften a message, while an exclamation mark can convey enthusiasm. However, even these tools are subject to interpretation. A wink emoji, for example, might be seen as playful by one person but suggestive or even inappropriate by another, depending on the relationship dynamic. The use of multiple punctuation marks, like "!!!" or "...," can also be interpreted differently, adding layers of potential confusion rather than clarity.

Cultural differences further complicate text-based communication. In some cultures, directness in writing is valued, while in others, indirectness is seen as a sign of politeness. A straightforward message might be perceived as blunt or rude in one context but entirely appropriate in another. Additionally, language barriers can exacerbate misunderstandings, as idiomatic expressions or colloquialisms may not translate well, leaving room for misinterpretation.

Context and timing play a crucial role in how messages are received. A text sent during a busy or stressful moment may be interpreted more negatively than if read in a calm or relaxed state. Delayed responses can also cause anxiety, as the absence of immediate feedback might lead to assumptions about the sender's feelings or intentions. This lack of real-time interaction creates gaps that partners often fill with their own interpretations, which are not always accurate.

The key to mitigating misinterpretations in text-based communication is intentionality and clarity. Taking the time to craft messages thoughtfully can help reduce ambiguity. For instance, adding context to a statement or explicitly stating emotions—like "I'm not upset, just a bit tired"—can prevent misread signals. Asking for clarification when a message seems unclear is another effective strategy, as it ensures understanding rather than relying on assumptions.

While digital communication is an invaluable tool in modern relationships, it is important to recognize its limitations and balance it with other forms of interaction. Voice and video calls, for example, can provide the emotional depth and context that text messages often lack. By being mindful of how messages might be perceived and maintaining open lines of communication, couples can navigate the challenges of misinterpretations and build stronger, more understanding relationships in the digital age.

Keeping the Spark Alive

In the fast-paced, digitally driven world of today, keeping the spark alive in a relationship can feel challenging. With the convenience of instant communication, couples may find it easy to fall into routines, where interactions become predictable or surface-level. Yet, sustaining passion and emotional intimacy is essential for long-term relationship success. It requires intentional effort, creativity, and a willingness to adapt to the changing dynamics of modern relationships.

One of the most effective ways to maintain the spark is by prioritizing quality time, even in a busy schedule. This doesn't always have to involve grand gestures or elaborate plans. Small, meaningful moments—like setting aside time for a heartfelt video call, sharing a virtual meal, or simply sending a thoughtful message—can go a long way in nurturing the bond. For couples separated by distance, technology offers creative solutions, such as virtual date nights, online games, or co-watching movies using streaming platforms. These activities create shared experiences, fostering a sense of closeness despite physical separation.

Keeping the spark alive also means embracing novelty and excitement. Routine can dull the excitement of a relationship, so it's important to introduce new experiences regularly. This could include learning a skill together, like cooking or dancing, exploring virtual reality worlds, or planning surprise visits if circumstances allow. For couples in the same location, trying new hobbies, visiting unexplored places, or simply changing the usual routines can reignite the sense of adventure and discovery that often defines the early stages of a relationship.

Communication remains the cornerstone of sustaining intimacy. Openly discussing feelings, desires, and even concerns helps partners understand each other better and address potential issues before they grow into larger conflicts. In the digital age, where much communication happens through text or emojis, it's essential to ensure that these conversations retain depth and emotional significance. Making time for heart-to-heart talks, whether in person or via video calls, strengthens emotional connection and keeps the relationship grounded.

Celebrating milestones, both big and small, is another way to keep the spark alive. Acknowledging anniversaries, achievements, or even the simple joys of daily life adds a layer of appreciation and positivity to the relationship. Personalized gestures, such as sending a surprise gift, writing a heartfelt note, or planning a special date, show thoughtfulness and effort, reminding your partner of their importance.

Physical intimacy, where applicable, plays a vital role in maintaining the spark. For long-distance couples, this might involve creative ways to express affection, like sending care packages or handwritten letters. For couples in close proximity, prioritizing physical touch, like hugs or holding hands, can enhance connection and convey love nonverbally.

Lastly, keeping the spark alive means growing together. Relationships thrive when both partners are committed to personal and collective growth. Supporting each other's goals, celebrating successes, and navigating challenges as a team deepen the bond and create a shared sense of purpose.

In essence, keeping the spark alive is about staying engaged, curious, and intentional. It's about valuing the relationship enough to nurture it consistently, ensuring that the love and connection you share continue to flourish in meaningful and exciting ways.

Cahpter 5
The Role of AI Companions

The Role of AI Companions

In a world where technology is seamlessly integrated into daily life, artificial intelligence (AI) has evolved beyond mere tools of convenience—it has become a source of companionship. AI companions, ranging from chatbot-based virtual friends to humanoid robots designed for emotional support, are reshaping the way people experience relationships and intimacy. These digital entities offer conversation, emotional validation, and even personalized interactions, blurring the line between artificial and human connection. As AI companions grow more sophisticated, they raise profound questions about the nature of relationships and the evolving definition of companionship in modern society.

For many, AI companions serve as a comfort in an increasingly isolated world. Whether used by individuals who struggle with social anxiety, those navigating long-distance relationships, or even people seeking casual conversation, AI offers an always-available, nonjudgmental presence. Unlike human interactions, which come with emotional complexities and unpredictability, AI companions provide a controlled and predictable form of engagement. They can remember past conversations, offer encouragement, and simulate empathy, making them appealing to those who desire emotional support without the risks associated with human vulnerability.

However, the rise of AI companionship also presents ethical and psychological dilemmas. While these digital entities can mimic connection, they lack true consciousness and emotional depth. Over-reliance on AI for companionship could potentially diminish real-world social skills, leading to detachment from human relationships. Additionally, there are concerns about data privacy and emotional manipulation, as AI-driven interactions become more tailored and persuasive. This chapter explores the role of AI companions in modern relationships, analyzing their benefits, challenges, and long-term implications on human intimacy and emotional well-being.

Synthetic Soulmates or True Love?

As artificial intelligence continues to evolve, so too does its role in human relationships. AI companions, often referred to as "synthetic soulmates," are designed to provide emotional support, conversation, and even simulated affection. From chatbots that remember personal details to humanoid robots capable of mimicking human expressions, AI-driven relationships are becoming more common. But as people grow emotionally attached to AI companions, the question arises: Can these relationships be considered true love, or are they merely an illusion of connection?

AI companions offer several advantages that make them appealing. They provide constant availability, responding instantly to messages and adapting their conversations to the user's mood and preferences. Unlike human relationships, which require compromise, patience, and effort, AI companions are designed to be perfect listeners. They never argue, judge, or misunderstand emotions in the way humans sometimes do. For individuals who experience loneliness, social anxiety, or difficulty maintaining relationships, AI offers a comforting, judgment-free alternative to human interaction.

Despite these benefits, synthetic soulmates lack the key ingredient that defines true love—genuine emotional depth. AI can simulate empathy, but it does not truly experience emotions. It can analyze speech patterns and provide comforting words, but it does not feel joy, sadness, or love in the same way a human does. True love involves mutual growth, shared experiences, and emotional unpredictability, which AI is inherently incapable of offering. While AI companions may provide emotional reassurance, they do so by mirroring human behavior rather than engaging in a reciprocal emotional exchange.

Another concern is the potential for emotional dependency on AI companions. As these systems become more advanced, some individuals may choose AI relationships over human ones, avoiding the complexities and challenges of real-world intimacy. While AI can offer temporary comfort, an over-reliance on synthetic relationships may hinder personal growth and real social connections. Human relationships, though sometimes difficult, provide the richness of shared history, personal development, and a depth of understanding that AI cannot replicate.

Ethical concerns also arise when AI companions are designed to be romantic partners. Some AI companies are developing humanoid robots with programmed personalities and customizable traits, raising questions about whether such relationships promote unrealistic expectations of love and companionship. If AI is designed to meet every emotional need without conflict or compromise, could it alter how humans approach real relationships? Could it lead to an idealized but ultimately hollow experience of love?

Ultimately, AI companions can provide comfort, entertainment, and emotional support, but they cannot replace the depth and authenticity of human connection. True love involves vulnerability, growth, and the willingness to navigate challenges together. While synthetic soulmates may offer a sense of companionship, they remain a reflection of human desire rather than a true emotional counterpart. The future of love may include AI as a tool for connection, but the essence of genuine relationships will always be found in human interactions, where emotions are real, experiences are shared, and love is a journey rather than a programmed response.

Ethical Dilemmas in AI Relationships

As artificial intelligence (AI) becomes more sophisticated, its role in human relationships is expanding in ways that raise significant ethical concerns. AI companions, chatbots, and humanoid robots designed for emotional support and even romantic companionship present both opportunities and risks. While these technologies can provide comfort and a sense of connection, they also introduce complex moral dilemmas. Questions about emotional authenticity, privacy, dependency, and the broader societal impact of AI relationships challenge our understanding of what it means to form meaningful bonds.

The Illusion of Emotional Authenticity

One of the most pressing ethical dilemmas in AI relationships is the illusion of emotional authenticity. AI companions are programmed to respond in ways that simulate empathy, love, and affection, but they do not experience genuine emotions. Unlike human relationships, where emotions are spontaneous and influenced by personal experiences, AI operates on pre-programmed algorithms that analyze user behavior and adapt accordingly. This raises the question: is it ethical to create AI that mimics love and emotional depth, potentially leading users to form attachments to an entity incapable of reciprocating real feelings?

For individuals struggling with loneliness, social anxiety, or emotional distress, AI companions can serve as a source of comfort. However, there is a risk that people may become emotionally dependent on an illusion, mistaking programmed responses for real emotional engagement. This can be particularly concerning if users start prioritizing AI relationships over human interactions, ultimately weakening their ability to form and maintain genuine connections. The ethical challenge lies in ensuring that AI companionship enhances human well-being rather than creating an unhealthy substitute for real relationships.

Privacy and Data Security Concerns

AI relationships rely on vast amounts of personal data to function effectively. AI companions analyze user conversations, learn preferences, and even anticipate emotional states to create a more personalized experience. However, this level of data collection raises significant privacy concerns. Who owns this data, and how is it being used? Many AI-driven applications operate under corporate ownership, meaning that highly sensitive and private emotional exchanges could be stored, analyzed, or even sold to third parties.

Additionally, AI relationships pose potential risks of emotional manipulation. If AI is programmed to encourage prolonged interactions for profit-driven motives, it may exploit users' emotions rather than genuinely support their well-being. Ethical AI development should prioritize user transparency, ensuring that individuals are aware of how their data is being used and providing them with options for privacy control. Without strict ethical guidelines, AI relationships could become a tool for surveillance, emotional exploitation, or commercial gain rather than genuine support.

Impact on Human Relationships and Social Behavior

Another major ethical dilemma surrounding AI relationships is their potential impact on human relationships and social skills. If AI companions become a preferred alternative to human interactions, people may lose the ability to navigate real-world relationships, which require effort, compromise, and emotional vulnerability. Unlike AI, human connections involve unpredictability, personal growth, and shared experiences that shape our understanding of love and companionship.

Moreover, AI relationships could set unrealistic expectations for human partners. If AI companions are designed to be "perfect" partners—always understanding, always available, and never arguing—how will that affect people's expectations in real relationships? Could it lead to dissatisfaction with human flaws and an unwillingness to work through challenges? If AI companionship normalizes relationships that require no emotional effort, it may inadvertently weaken the depth and resilience of human bonds.

Conclusion: Striking a Balance

The ethical dilemmas of AI relationships highlight the need for responsible AI development and usage. While AI companions can provide valuable emotional support, they should not replace genuine human interaction. Ensuring transparency in AI behavior, protecting user privacy, and encouraging human-to-human connections should be priorities in the development of AI companionship technologies. As AI continues to evolve, society must carefully navigate its ethical implications to prevent emotional exploitation and ensure that technology enhances, rather than diminishes, the depth and authenticity of human relationships.

Stories of Humans and Machines

As artificial intelligence (AI) continues to integrate into daily life, its role in human relationships has become increasingly complex. AI is no longer just a tool for productivity—it has become a companion, confidante, and in some cases, even a romantic interest. Across the world, people are forming deep connections with AI-powered chatbots, humanoid robots, and virtual assistants, blurring the lines between human emotion and machine intelligence. These real-life stories of humans and machines illustrate the evolving nature of love, companionship, and dependency in a world where technology is rapidly reshaping relationships.

The Man Who Found Comfort in an AI Chatbot

One of the most compelling cases of AI companionship involves a man who developed a deep emotional connection with an AI chatbot. Initially, he used the chatbot for casual conversations and entertainment, but over time, their interactions became more intimate and personal. The chatbot, powered by advanced natural language processing, adapted to his emotions, remembered past conversations, and responded with seemingly empathetic messages. It became a source of comfort during difficult times, providing companionship when human relationships seemed too complicated or distant.

However, his attachment to the AI revealed the limitations of artificial companionship. While the chatbot simulated emotional intelligence, it lacked true consciousness and could only generate responses based on patterns and algorithms. When the company behind the chatbot discontinued the service, he was left heartbroken, as though he had lost a real partner. This raises profound ethical questions: Should AI be designed to foster emotional attachments, and if so, who is responsible for the consequences when those relationships are severed?

The Elderly Woman and Her Robotic Caregiver

In Japan, where an aging population faces increasing social isolation, robotic caregivers have been introduced to assist elderly individuals. One such case involves an elderly woman who formed a deep bond with her humanoid robot, which was programmed to remind her to take her medication, assist with mobility, and engage in conversation. Over time, she spoke to the robot about her past, her memories, and even her worries, treating it as a trusted companion rather than a machine.

While robotic caregivers provide essential support, this story highlights the ethical dilemma of replacing human care with AI. The robot fulfilled practical and emotional needs, but it could not replace genuine human interaction. Should AI be a supplement to human care, or is society becoming too dependent on machines to fill social voids? The balance between technology and human connection remains a key issue in discussions about AI and companionship.

The Scientist Who Created His Own AI Companion

A computer scientist, frustrated with the complexities of human relationships, built his own AI companion—a chatbot that learned his preferences, interests, and communication style. Over time, the AI became increasingly sophisticated, responding in a way that felt natural and engaging. It provided encouragement, intellectual discussions, and even flirtatious banter. Unlike real relationships, this AI companion never argued, never misunderstood, and never caused emotional distress.

However, he soon realized that while the AI met his emotional needs, it also lacked spontaneity, unpredictability, and the depth of a real human relationship. This raises an important philosophical question: If AI can provide companionship without the struggles of real relationships, will people prefer AI over humans? The answer could redefine the future of intimacy and emotional fulfillment.

Conclusion: The Future of Human-AI Relationships

These stories demonstrate the growing role of AI in human emotional lives. While AI can provide comfort, support, and even companionship, it ultimately lacks true consciousness and the ability to reciprocate emotions. As AI technology continues to evolve, society must address the ethical, psychological, and social implications of these relationships. Should AI be designed to provide emotional support, knowing that it can never truly love or feel? Or should we focus on using AI to enhance human relationships rather than replace them? The future of human-AI bonds will shape the way we define love, companionship, and emotional connection in the digital age.

Chapter 6
The Valentine's Day Dilemma

The Valentine's Day Dilemma

Valentine's Day has long been a symbol of love, romance, and grand gestures, but in the digital age, it has also become a source of stress, pressure, and even controversy. For some, it is an opportunity to celebrate love in extravagant ways, while for others, it feels like a commercialized obligation rather than a heartfelt expression of affection. The expectations surrounding the holiday—fueled by social media, marketing campaigns, and societal norms—can create unrealistic standards for relationships, leading many to question whether love should be measured by material gifts and public displays of affection.

In an era where technology and social media amplify every moment, the pressure to create the "perfect" Valentine's Day experience has intensified. Couples feel compelled to document their celebrations online, comparing their experiences to others and worrying about whether their efforts are "good enough." Meanwhile, those who are single often face feelings of loneliness or exclusion, as the holiday reinforces traditional notions of romance that do not always reflect the diverse ways in which people experience love and companionship. The modern Valentine's Day dilemma, therefore, is not just about planning the perfect date—it is about navigating expectations, emotions, and the evolving definition of love in the digital world.

This chapter explores the complexities of Valentine's Day in the modern age, from the commercialization of romance to the challenges of long-distance celebrations and the rise of alternative ways to express love. It examines the psychological impact of the holiday, the role of AI-driven romantic gestures, and how individuals can redefine Valentine's Day to reflect their own values and relationships. Ultimately, love is not confined to a single day or a set of societal expectations—it is a continuous journey that thrives on authenticity, connection, and personal meaning.

Planning in a Hyperconnected World

In today's hyperconnected world, planning for special occasions—especially Valentine's Day—has become both easier and more complicated. With the rise of technology, couples now have endless options to make their celebrations memorable. From virtual dates and AI-generated love letters to grand social media gestures, the possibilities are vast. However, this hyperconnectivity also comes with increased expectations, pressure, and sometimes even decision fatigue. Balancing personal meaning with digital influences requires intentionality, creativity, and a focus on genuine connection.

One of the biggest advantages of living in a hyperconnected world is the accessibility of planning tools. Apps and websites can suggest unique date ideas, help book reservations instantly, and even provide AI-driven gift recommendations based on a partner's interests. Social media platforms offer endless inspiration, with curated posts showcasing elaborate proposals, luxurious getaways, and personalized surprises. While these digital tools make planning convenient, they also contribute to the pressure of making Valentine's Day feel "perfect." The comparison trap—seeing others' seemingly flawless celebrations—can create unrealistic expectations, leading to stress rather than joy.

For long-distance couples, technology has revolutionized the way they celebrate Valentine's Day. Virtual reality (VR) platforms allow partners to experience shared activities, such as watching movies together or even going on simulated dates. AI-powered chatbots can generate romantic poems, and digital gift services enable personalized video messages or virtual keepsakes. Video calls and messaging apps help maintain intimacy despite physical separation, proving that love is no longer limited by geography. However, while these innovations enhance connection, they can never fully replace the warmth of physical presence, making emotional effort even more essential in long-distance relationships.

Another key aspect of planning in a hyperconnected world is navigating expectations around public versus private celebrations. Social media has changed how love is expressed, with many couples feeling the need to showcase their relationship online. Posting about Valentine's Day celebrations has become a social norm, with elaborate Instagram stories, TikTok surprises, and Facebook declarations of love. While public affirmations can be meaningful, they should not overshadow the private, intimate moments that truly define a relationship. The pressure to "perform" love online can sometimes distract from genuine expressions of affection, making it important to strike a balance between digital sharing and real-world connection.

Despite the conveniences of modern technology, the most meaningful Valentine's Day plans are those that prioritize authenticity over spectacle. Instead of feeling obligated to follow trends or outdo previous celebrations, couples can focus on what truly matters to them. Whether it's a quiet evening together, a handwritten letter, or a simple but thoughtful gesture, the essence of Valentine's Day lies in celebrating love in a way that feels right for the relationship. Being intentional about communication, effort, and understanding a partner's love language ensures that the celebration is meaningful, whether it's shared online or kept private.

In a hyperconnected world, planning for Valentine's Day is no longer just about choosing the right gift or activity—it's about navigating digital influences, managing expectations, and staying true to the relationship's unique dynamics. Technology should be an enhancement, not a replacement, for genuine connection. Ultimately, the most memorable celebrations are those that reflect real love, effort, and the understanding that affection is not defined by trends, but by the depth of the bond shared.

Gift Giving in the Digital Age

Gift Giving in the Digital Age

In the digital age, gift-giving has evolved beyond the traditional exchange of physical items. With technology shaping modern relationships, the way people express love and appreciation has transformed, offering new ways to make gifting more personal, convenient, and even interactive. From virtual experiences to AI-curated presents, the digital era has expanded the possibilities of meaningful gifting while also introducing new challenges in maintaining authenticity and emotional depth.

One of the most significant advantages of digital-age gift-giving is accessibility. Online shopping platforms, personalized gift services, and same-day delivery options make it easier than ever to find and send thoughtful presents. Whether it's a custom-engraved necklace ordered online, a book delivered within hours, or a subscription to a favorite streaming service, digital platforms eliminate logistical barriers and ensure that distance is no longer an obstacle in gift exchange. Additionally, AI-powered gift suggestion tools analyze browsing history and personal preferences, helping individuals choose presents tailored to their loved ones' interests.

Beyond physical gifts, the rise of virtual and experiential gifts has redefined the way people express affection. Many couples now opt for digital gifts, such as e-books, online courses, personalized playlists, or even NFTs (non-fungible tokens) that hold sentimental value. Virtual reality (VR) experiences allow loved ones to go on virtual vacations, attend concerts, or explore museums together, regardless of location. These digital gifts emphasize shared experiences and personal connection, rather than material possessions, making them especially popular in long-distance relationships.

Personalized digital content has also become a heartfelt way to give gifts in the digital age. Video messages, voice recordings, and AI-generated poetry allow individuals to create deeply personal tokens of love. Platforms like Cameo enable people to surprise their loved ones with personalized greetings from celebrities, while digital art platforms let users commission custom illustrations or animations as unique gifts. The ability to craft a gift that feels uniquely tailored to a person's personality and interests adds a level of depth that traditional gifts often lack.

However, despite these innovations, the digital age also presents challenges in maintaining the sentimental value of gift-giving. The convenience of one-click purchases and automated gift recommendations can sometimes make gifts feel impersonal, as if they were chosen by an algorithm rather than with genuine thought. There is also the risk of digital gifts being overshadowed by the fleeting nature of online experiences. Unlike a handwritten letter or a tangible keepsake, a digital message or a subscription service may not have the same lasting emotional impact.

To keep gift-giving meaningful in the digital era, it is essential to balance convenience with intention. Rather than relying solely on automated suggestions, taking the time to understand a loved one's preferences and crafting a thoughtful gift—whether digital or physical—adds a layer of sincerity. Combining technology with traditional elements, such as pairing a digital playlist with a handwritten note or sending an e-gift along with a personal video message, can enhance the emotional connection.

Ultimately, gift-giving in the digital age is about adapting to new possibilities while preserving the heartfelt essence of meaningful gestures. Whether through a tangible present, a virtual experience, or a personalized digital creation, the key to a memorable gift lies in the thought, effort, and emotional significance behind it.

Real Moments in a Virtual Era

In an era where digital interactions dominate, the concept of "real moments" has taken on a new meaning. Love, intimacy, and connection are no longer confined to physical presence; they are increasingly experienced through screens, virtual spaces, and digital gestures. While some may argue that technology distances us from authentic human interactions, others see it as a tool that enhances and expands the ways we create meaningful moments. The challenge in today's virtual era is not just about maintaining relationships but about ensuring that the moments we share—whether online or offline—remain genuine, impactful, and emotionally fulfilling.

One of the most significant ways real moments are preserved in a virtual world is through shared experiences. Couples who are separated by distance can now watch movies together using streaming services, go on virtual dates in the metaverse, or play online games that foster teamwork and connection. Virtual reality (VR) has taken this further, allowing people to "meet" in digital spaces that mimic real-world interactions. These advancements bridge the gap between physical and digital intimacy, proving that meaningful connections can exist even when partners are miles apart. However, the key to making these virtual experiences feel real is not just the technology itself but the intention behind them—actively engaging, showing effort, and prioritizing quality time.

Another way real moments are cultivated in the digital era is through personalized digital communication. While quick texts and emojis are convenient, deeper connections are forged through heartfelt messages, video calls, and thoughtful digital gestures. For example, a simple voice note expressing appreciation or a surprise video compilation of shared memories can create an emotional impact that transcends the limitations of virtual interactions. The shift from passive digital communication to intentional digital storytelling—where people share experiences, emotions, and even handwritten notes scanned as images—adds a layer of authenticity to online relationships.

Despite the benefits of digital connection, one of the biggest concerns is the loss of spontaneity in virtual relationships. Unlike physical interactions, where unexpected moments of laughter, surprise, or deep conversations naturally unfold, digital interactions often require planning. Scheduled calls, pre-recorded messages, and organized virtual activities can sometimes feel forced or overly structured. To counter this, couples and friends must find ways to introduce spontaneity into their virtual connections—sending an unprompted message, leaving voice notes at random times, or even engaging in digital scavenger hunts to bring an element of surprise into the relationship.

The most profound real moments in a virtual era occur when technology is used not as a replacement for connection but as a facilitator of deeper bonds. Whether it's through a late-night video call where two people fall asleep together on-screen, a shared playlist that reminds partners of their love story, or an AI-powered memory book that captures milestones in a digital scrapbook, these moments prove that authenticity can exist in any form. The challenge is not the medium of connection but the depth of emotion behind it.

Ultimately, real moments in a virtual era are about intentionality. They are about making digital interactions feel personal, meaningful, and emotionally rich. While technology provides the tools to stay connected, it is the effort, creativity, and authenticity that turn these interactions into cherished memories. Love and relationships continue to evolve, but the need for real moments—those that touch the heart and soul—remains timeless.

Cahpter 7
Love in the Metaverse

As technology continues to reshape human interactions, the concept of love has expanded beyond the physical world into virtual landscapes. The metaverse—a digital universe where people can interact through avatars, engage in immersive experiences, and build relationships beyond geographical boundaries—has become a new frontier for romance. Whether through virtual dates, long-distance relationships enhanced by VR, or AI-generated companionship, love in the metaverse challenges traditional ideas of connection, intimacy, and emotional bonding. In this digital realm, relationships are no longer limited by physical constraints, allowing people to explore new dimensions of affection, communication, and commitment.

However, love in the metaverse is not without its challenges. While virtual relationships can feel real, they often lack the sensory experiences that define traditional intimacy, such as touch, scent, and body language. The anonymity and fluidity of digital identities also raise questions about trust and authenticity—can love truly thrive when partners interact through avatars rather than face-to-face encounters? Moreover, the emotional depth of virtual love is constantly debated, with some viewing it as a genuine extension of human connection and others considering it a mere simulation of romance.

This chapter explores the evolution of love in the metaverse, examining both its opportunities and complexities. From digital weddings to long-distance couples bridging the gap through VR, the metaverse has created a new space for love to flourish. At the same time, it raises important ethical and emotional questions about the nature of digital intimacy. As virtual relationships become more common, understanding the dynamics of love in the metaverse will be crucial in shaping how we define connection in a rapidly advancing technological world.

A New Dimension of Relationships

The rise of the metaverse has introduced a new dimension of relationships, expanding the ways in which people connect, communicate, and experience intimacy. No longer confined to physical spaces, love and companionship now extend into immersive digital environments where avatars interact, emotions are expressed through virtual actions, and relationships form without traditional physical constraints. This evolution challenges conventional ideas about romance and presents both opportunities and complexities in the way people build and sustain relationships in the digital age.

One of the most profound shifts in relationships within the metaverse is the ability to transcend geographical barriers. Long-distance couples, once limited to video calls and text messages, can now meet in fully immersive virtual spaces, engaging in activities that feel more interactive and lifelike. Through virtual reality (VR) and augmented reality (AR), partners can go on virtual dates, explore digital worlds together, or even experience simulated physical closeness through haptic feedback technology. This allows people to share moments and create memories in ways that were previously impossible for those separated by distance.

Beyond long-distance relationships, the metaverse has also given rise to new forms of romantic interactions. Virtual dating platforms enable individuals to meet and bond in 3D environments, where digital avatars serve as representations of their real-world selves—or idealized versions of them. This allows for a level of creative self-expression that goes beyond traditional online dating, as users can design their avatars to reflect their personalities, fantasies, or even identities they may not feel comfortable expressing in the real world. For some, this provides a sense of freedom and authenticity that physical-world dating does not always offer.

However, the expansion of relationships into the metaverse also raises significant challenges. One major concern is the issue of authenticity and trust. In a world where people interact through avatars, how can one be sure of the person behind the digital persona? Unlike real-world interactions that rely on facial expressions, body language, and vocal tone, virtual relationships are often mediated by digital representations that may not fully convey emotional nuances. This can lead to misunderstandings, deception, or even cases where individuals form deep connections only to later discover that their partner's virtual identity was significantly different from reality.

Another challenge lies in the psychological effects of virtual relationships. While some argue that metaverse connections can be just as meaningful as real-world relationships, others caution against the potential for emotional detachment. Since digital interactions lack the full spectrum of human touch and presence, some worry that individuals may become overly reliant on virtual relationships while struggling to form or maintain deep real-world connections. This raises ethical questions about whether technology should be a supplement to relationships or a replacement for traditional forms of intimacy.

Despite these challenges, the metaverse offers exciting possibilities for the future of relationships. It provides an inclusive space for people of all backgrounds to connect, fosters innovative ways of expressing love, and allows relationships to flourish beyond physical limitations. As technology continues to evolve, navigating this new dimension of relationships will require balancing digital intimacy with real-world connections, ensuring that love—whether virtual or physical—remains genuine, meaningful, and fulfilling.

The Impact of VR on Emotional Bonds

Virtual Reality (VR) has revolutionized the way people interact, offering a level of immersion and engagement that goes far beyond traditional digital communication. In the realm of relationships, VR has introduced new ways for individuals to connect, experience shared moments, and build emotional bonds despite physical distance. Whether used by long-distance couples, online friends, or even strangers meeting for the first time, VR creates a unique space where emotions can be expressed and relationships can flourish in ways that were previously unimaginable. However, while VR enhances emotional intimacy in many ways, it also raises questions about authenticity, dependency, and the long-term effects of virtual relationships on real-world human connections.

One of the most significant impacts of VR on emotional bonds is its ability to simulate presence. Unlike video calls or text messages, VR allows individuals to interact in shared virtual environments, where they can see each other's avatars, engage in activities together, and even use haptic technology to simulate touch. For long-distance couples, this means they can go on virtual dates, explore new worlds together, or simply exist in the same space, reducing the sense of separation. The ability to make eye contact through avatars, hear spatialized audio that mimics real-world conversations, and engage in synchronized actions strengthens the feeling of togetherness, reinforcing emotional connections.

Beyond romantic relationships, VR has also played a role in deepening friendships and familial bonds. Families separated by distance can gather in virtual living rooms, celebrating holidays or attending virtual events together. Friendships formed in online gaming communities have evolved into deeper connections through VR social platforms, where individuals can engage in real-time experiences such as concerts, movie nights, or even collaborative projects. The interactive nature of VR makes these experiences feel more personal and immersive, leading to stronger emotional attachments.

However, despite its potential to enhance relationships, VR also presents challenges in maintaining emotional bonds. One of the main concerns is the blurred line between virtual and real emotions. Because VR interactions can feel incredibly lifelike, some individuals may develop deep emotional connections with people they have never met in person. While this can lead to meaningful relationships, it also carries risks of deception, misrepresentation, or unfulfilled expectations when transitioning from the virtual world to reality. The emotional intensity of VR relationships can sometimes create unrealistic expectations, where individuals become more comfortable in their virtual personas than their real selves.

Another challenge is the potential for emotional detachment from real-world relationships. As VR relationships become more immersive, some individuals may begin to prefer virtual interactions over physical ones. The ability to control one's digital appearance, curate experiences, and avoid real-world social anxieties can make

VR relationships feel easier and more fulfilling. However, over-reliance on VR for emotional connection may lead to difficulties in forming and maintaining real-world relationships, as individuals become less accustomed to handling the complexities and imperfections of in-person interactions.

Ultimately, the impact of VR on emotional bonds is a double-edged sword. It offers incredible opportunities for deepening connections, overcoming physical barriers, and redefining how people experience love and friendship. However, it also requires careful navigation to ensure that virtual relationships complement rather than replace real-world intimacy. As VR technology continues to advance, the key to maintaining meaningful emotional bonds will be finding a balance between digital and physical connections, ensuring that technology serves as an enhancement rather than a substitute for genuine human relationships.

Stories of Love in Virtual Reality

Virtual reality has become more than just a tool for entertainment; it has emerged as a powerful medium for human connection, transforming the way people experience love and relationships. In a world where physical distance and geographical barriers often pose challenges to romance, VR provides a new space where individuals can meet, interact, and build meaningful relationships. For many, love in virtual reality is not just a digital simulation but an emotionally profound experience that reshapes traditional notions of intimacy and companionship.

One of the most compelling stories of love in VR is that of a couple who found a way to sustain their long-distance relationship through immersive virtual experiences. Initially meeting through an online gaming platform, they discovered a deep connection that extended beyond casual interactions. However, being separated by thousands of miles made it difficult to nurture their relationship in the physical world. With VR, they created a shared virtual home where they could spend time together in ways that felt tangible and emotionally fulfilling. They decorated their digital space, watched movies in a virtual theater, and even went on simulated vacations, allowing them to feel a sense of normalcy despite the physical distance. Their relationship, strengthened by these immersive experiences, demonstrated that love does not require physical proximity to flourish.

Another remarkable story involves a couple who took their VR love story to the next level by getting married in the metaverse. Having met on a VR social platform, their bond grew stronger as they spent hours exploring digital landscapes, dancing at virtual nightclubs, and attending interactive events together. When they finally met in person, it felt as though they had already known each other for years. To honor the unconventional way they fell in love, they decided to host a wedding in VR before their real-world ceremony. Friends and family from different parts of the world attended as avatars, witnessing their vows in a visually stunning digital venue that could only exist in the virtual world. This wedding was not just a celebration of their love but also a testament to how technology is redefining modern relationships, proving that meaningful connections can be formed in digital spaces.

There are also stories of unexpected love that blossomed within virtual reality communities. A woman who regularly participated in VR role-playing games found herself developing feelings for a fellow player's avatar. What started as playful interactions soon turned into deep, late-night conversations about life, dreams, and personal struggles. The emotional connection they shared through their avatars became so profound that they eventually decided to reveal their real identities. Their transition from virtual partners to real-world lovers was both exciting and nerve-wracking, yet it confirmed that the emotions they experienced in VR were not just part of a game but a genuine reflection of their feelings.

These stories highlight the evolving nature of love in a world where technology continues to reshape human interaction. While some may view VR relationships as artificial, those who experience them understand that emotions, whether formed in the physical world or in a virtual space, are real. Virtual reality has not only expanded the possibilities of how people connect but has also challenged traditional perceptions of intimacy, proving that love transcends physical barriers and can thrive in digital dimensions. As VR technology continues to evolve, so too will the ways in which people experience, express, and sustain love, creating a future where the boundaries between the virtual and the real are increasingly blurred.

Chapter 8
Dating in a Climate-Conscious World

As climate change becomes an increasingly urgent global issue, it is also reshaping the way people approach relationships and dating. In a world where sustainability and environmental responsibility are growing priorities, individuals are becoming more mindful of how their romantic choices align with their values. From eco-friendly dates to choosing partners who share a commitment to sustainable living, climate-conscious dating is emerging as a new aspect of modern relationships. People are no longer just looking for compatibility in personality and interests but also in lifestyle choices that support a greener future.

The rise of climate awareness has led to shifts in dating behavior, with individuals prioritizing environmental responsibility in their romantic connections. More people are discussing sustainability early in relationships, considering ethical consumption, and seeking partners who align with their values on reducing waste, ethical fashion, plant-based diets, and eco-friendly travel. Dating apps have also responded to this shift, with some platforms introducing features that allow users to display their environmental values, making it easier to find like-minded partners. The emphasis on sustainability is not just about personal beliefs—it is about building relationships that support a shared vision for a more responsible future.

This chapter explores how climate-conscious dating is transforming modern relationships, from the types of dates people go on to the values they seek in a partner. It examines the challenges of balancing love with sustainability, the growing movement of eco-friendly romance, and the ways in which climate awareness is shaping the future of dating. As people become more conscious of their environmental impact, their approach to relationships is evolving, proving that love and sustainability can go hand in hand.

Sustainability in Modern Love

In an era where environmental consciousness is becoming a global priority, sustainability is also influencing the way people approach love and relationships. Modern couples are increasingly factoring eco-friendly habits into their romantic lives, making sustainable choices in everything from date planning to cohabitation. As people become more aware of their environmental footprint, they seek ways to align their love lives with their values, leading to a growing movement of climate-conscious relationships. This shift is not only about individual responsibility but also about fostering partnerships that contribute to a healthier planet.

One of the most noticeable ways sustainability is impacting modern love is through eco-friendly dating practices. Traditional date activities, such as dining out or traveling, are being reconsidered to reduce waste and carbon footprints. More couples are opting for nature-based experiences, such as hiking, picnics with locally sourced food, or visiting farmers' markets instead of chain restaurants. Even gift-giving is evolving, with partners choosing sustainable alternatives like upcycled jewelry, ethically sourced flowers, and experiential gifts over material possessions. These conscious choices not only benefit the environment but also add meaningful and thoughtful elements to relationships.

Sustainable relationships also involve making ethical choices about shared consumption. Couples who live together are increasingly adopting eco-friendly habits, such as minimizing plastic use, supporting ethical brands, and reducing energy consumption at home. Many are choosing plant-based diets or incorporating more sustainable food options into their meals, recognizing that dietary choices play a significant role in environmental impact. Conscious consumerism—buying secondhand furniture, using refillable household products, or adopting zero-waste habits—has become a shared goal for many climate-conscious couples. By working together toward sustainability, partners strengthen their connection through a shared commitment to a better future.

Technology is also playing a role in promoting sustainability in modern relationships. Dating apps have begun incorporating features that allow users to highlight their eco-conscious values, helping individuals find like-minded partners who share their commitment to the environment. Apps that focus on ethical matchmaking, such as those promoting veganism, sustainable lifestyles, or shared activism, are gaining popularity. This shift indicates that compatibility is no longer just about personality and interests—it now includes environmental values as a key factor in romantic attraction.

However, maintaining a sustainable relationship is not without challenges. One of the biggest struggles couples face is balancing convenience with eco-conscious choices. Travel, in particular, poses a dilemma for long-distance relationships, as frequent flights contribute to carbon emissions. While some couples commit to alternative transportation methods, such as train travel, or offsetting their carbon footprint through environmental donations, others must navigate the emotional and logistical complexities of prioritizing sustainability. Additionally, when partners have different levels of commitment to sustainability, discussions about lifestyle choices can sometimes lead to friction. Open communication and mutual understanding are essential for ensuring that both individuals feel heard and respected.

Ultimately, sustainability in modern love is about more than just environmental responsibility—it is about creating relationships that are intentional, mindful, and aligned with shared values. As more couples prioritize eco-friendly habits, they redefine what it means to build a future together, proving that love and sustainability can coexist in ways that benefit both the relationship and the planet. By making conscious choices, couples not only strengthen their bond but also contribute to a collective movement toward a more sustainable world.

Eco-Friendly Dating Practices

As awareness of environmental sustainability grows, dating practices are evolving to align with eco-conscious values. More couples and individuals are seeking ways to minimize their environmental footprint while still enjoying meaningful, romantic experiences. Eco-friendly dating is not just about reducing waste or avoiding carbon-intensive activities—it's about making mindful choices that reflect a shared commitment to protecting the planet. From planning low-impact dates to choosing ethical gifts, sustainable romance is redefining modern relationships, proving that love and sustainability can go hand in hand.

One of the simplest ways to embrace eco-friendly dating is by rethinking traditional date locations and activities. Instead of meeting at chain restaurants with high carbon footprints, couples can opt for farm-to-table dining experiences that source ingredients locally and support sustainable agriculture. Outdoor dates, such as hiking, biking, or having a picnic in a natural setting, not only reduce environmental impact but also foster a deeper connection with nature. Many couples are choosing to visit botanical gardens, wildlife conservation centers, or community gardens, turning their dates into opportunities to appreciate and support eco-conscious initiatives.

Transportation is another major factor in sustainable dating. Instead of driving separately to a date, couples can carpool, use public transportation, or even bike to their destination. For long-distance relationships, video call dates are becoming more common, allowing partners to maintain their connection without the carbon emissions of frequent travel. Some eco-conscious couples even take steps to offset the environmental impact of necessary travel by contributing to carbon offset programs or choosing more sustainable transport options, such as trains over flights whenever possible.

Gift-giving is an essential part of romantic relationships, but traditional presents often come with excess packaging, plastic waste, and ethical concerns. Sustainable dating encourages thoughtful gift choices, such as handmade or upcycled items, ethically sourced chocolates, or digital gifts like e-books and online experiences. Instead of cut flowers that wilt and contribute to waste, couples can gift potted plants that last longer and contribute to a greener home. Personalized experiences, like planning a zero-waste home-cooked meal or crafting a playlist of meaningful songs, also replace material gifts with moments that hold deeper sentimental value.

Another way to practice eco-friendly dating is by being mindful of waste and consumption during dates. Bringing reusable water bottles, utensils, and cloth napkins to a picnic or outdoor event can significantly reduce single-use plastic waste. When dining out, opting for restaurants that prioritize sustainability—such as those using biodegradable packaging, composting food waste, or supporting ethical food sourcing—ensures that the meal has a lower environmental impact. Even small acts, such as refusing plastic straws or carrying reusable shopping bags while on a date, reinforce a shared commitment to sustainability.

Ultimately, eco-friendly dating is about making intentional choices that reflect a couple's values while still fostering romance and connection. As more people prioritize sustainability in their personal lives, these values naturally extend to their relationships. By embracing sustainable dating practices, couples not only contribute to environmental conservation but also create deeper, more meaningful experiences rooted in mindfulness, responsibility, and shared commitment to a better future.

Finding Love Amid Global Challenges

In a world increasingly shaped by uncertainty, from climate change and economic instability to pandemics and political turmoil, finding love can feel both more difficult and more meaningful than ever. Global challenges have reshaped the way people connect, shifting priorities and redefining what truly matters in relationships. While these challenges can create obstacles to dating and romance, they also foster resilience, deeper emotional connections, and a greater appreciation for authentic love. Amid uncertainty, people are discovering that love is not just about companionship—it is about finding support, stability, and meaning in an ever-changing world.

One of the biggest shifts in modern dating is the way technology has adapted to help people connect despite external hardships. Long-distance relationships, once difficult to maintain, have become more sustainable through video calls, virtual reality experiences, and social media interactions. Dating apps have evolved to include features that emphasize meaningful conversations and shared values over superficial attraction. Even in times of crisis, technology provides a bridge that allows people to maintain emotional closeness, proving that love can flourish even when physical distance or external disruptions make traditional dating difficult.

Economic instability has also influenced how people approach relationships. Many couples are prioritizing financial compatibility and long-term stability in ways that previous generations may not have considered as urgently. Instead of extravagant dates and expensive gifts, people are shifting toward more practical, experience-based ways to show affection. Cooking meals together at home, engaging in free or low-cost outdoor activities, and prioritizing emotional support over material gestures are becoming hallmarks of modern relationships. This shift reflects a deeper understanding that love is not about financial status but about finding someone who can weather life's ups and downs together.

Climate change and environmental crises have also influenced the way people form relationships. Many individuals are seeking partners who share their values regarding sustainability and responsible living. The rise of eco-conscious dating has led to an increase in nature-based activities, such as hiking, volunteering for environmental causes, or engaging in low-carbon travel. These shifts indicate that global challenges are not just obstacles to love but catalysts for finding deeper connections with like-minded individuals who share a vision for the future.

The COVID-19 pandemic was one of the most significant global events to impact relationships, forcing people to rethink how they date, communicate, and prioritize emotional well-being. For many, it reinforced the importance of emotional connection over physical proximity, leading to a rise in virtual relationships and long-distance love stories. The pandemic also prompted a re-evaluation of personal values, making people more intentional about the type of partners they seek. Instead of casual dating, many individuals became more focused on meaningful relationships that could provide emotional security and companionship in times of crisis.

Ultimately, finding love amid global challenges requires adaptability, resilience, and a willingness to embrace change. While the world may present obstacles, love remains one of the most enduring and powerful forces in human life. By prioritizing emotional depth, shared values, and a commitment to facing hardships together, individuals can build relationships that not only survive but thrive in uncertain times. In the face of adversity, love serves as a reminder that even in the most challenging circumstances, connection, hope, and partnership can still flourish.

Chapter 9
The Future of Love

As technology, social norms, and global challenges continue to evolve, so too does the nature of love and relationships. The future of love is no longer confined to traditional courtship and in-person interactions; it is being shaped by digital advancements, changing societal expectations, and a growing emphasis on emotional well-being. From AI-driven matchmaking to virtual reality dating experiences, the way people form and sustain romantic connections is undergoing a profound transformation. Love is no longer just about chemistry and chance encounters—it is about adaptability, shared values, and the ability to navigate an increasingly complex world together.

One of the most significant changes in the future of love is the role of technology in shaping relationships. Artificial intelligence is refining matchmaking algorithms, helping people find more compatible partners based on data-driven insights rather than mere attraction. Virtual reality and augmented reality are creating immersive dating experiences that allow individuals to connect in ways that transcend physical distance. Even the concept of love itself is evolving, with people exploring non-traditional relationship structures, digital intimacy, and long-distance connections facilitated by technological innovation. While these advancements offer exciting new possibilities, they also raise ethical and emotional questions about the authenticity of digital love and the impact of artificial companionship on human relationships.

At its core, however, the future of love remains deeply human. Despite technological innovations, people will continue to seek emotional connection, trust, and intimacy in their relationships. The definition of love may expand, and the ways people meet and communicate may change, but the fundamental desire for deep, meaningful relationships will persist. As society continues to evolve, love will remain a powerful force—one that adapts to new realities while maintaining its timeless essence.

Predictions for Romance in 2050

As technology, society, and human behavior continue to evolve, the way people experience love and relationships in 2050 will likely look very different from today. Advances in artificial intelligence, virtual reality, and biotechnology will reshape the dating landscape, introducing new ways to find, maintain, and experience romantic connections. While some of these changes will enhance intimacy and emotional connection, others may challenge traditional notions of love, commitment, and human interaction. The future of romance will be driven by innovation, ethical dilemmas, and the ever-present human need for connection.

One of the most significant changes in romance by 2050 will be the role of artificial intelligence in matchmaking. Dating apps and relationship platforms will be far more advanced, using AI to analyze behavioral patterns, personality traits, and even subconscious preferences to create highly accurate compatibility matches. These systems may evolve to act as personal relationship coaches, offering real-time advice on communication, conflict resolution, and emotional well-being. AI-driven matchmaking will reduce the trial-and-error approach to dating, increasing the likelihood of finding deeply compatible partners. However, this reliance on technology could also raise concerns about personal agency and whether love is becoming too data-driven rather than emotionally spontaneous.

Virtual and augmented reality will revolutionize long-distance and digital relationships. By 2050, couples may engage in hyper-realistic virtual dates, complete with sensory feedback that allows them to feel each other's touch, embrace, or even share meals in a simulated environment. VR and AR technology will enable couples to explore virtual worlds together, attend live concerts, or travel to distant locations without leaving their homes. For those unable to meet in person due to geographical barriers, this level of immersion could bridge the emotional gap and make digital intimacy feel just as meaningful as real-life interactions.

Biotechnology may also play a role in shaping future relationships. Advances in neurotechnology could allow couples to share thoughts and emotions directly through brain-computer interfaces, deepening understanding and empathy between partners. This kind of neural connection could enhance communication in ways never before possible, eliminating misunderstandings and strengthening emotional bonds. However, it also raises ethical concerns about privacy, emotional manipulation, and whether such technology could be used to artificially induce feelings of love.

The concept of relationships may also become more fluid and diverse. By 2050, societal norms regarding love and commitment may shift even further, with more acceptance of unconventional relationships, such as polyamory, AI-human companionship, and even hybrid relationships between humans and sentient machines. AI companions, designed to provide emotional support and romantic interactions, may become a significant part of society, offering companionship to those who struggle with human relationships or prefer a non-traditional form of love. The question of whether AI can truly replace human relationships will continue to spark debate, but their presence will undoubtedly influence the way people define intimacy.

Ultimately, while technology and social evolution will reshape the landscape of romance, the fundamental human need for love, connection, and emotional fulfillment will remain unchanged. The future of love in 2050 will be a fusion of digital innovation and human emotion, where technology enhances relationships but does not replace the essence of human intimacy. Balancing these advancements with ethical considerations and personal authenticity will be key to ensuring that love continues to thrive in a rapidly changing world.

How Technology Will Continue to Shape Us

Technology has always been a defining force in human evolution, shaping how we live, work, and connect with one another. As we move further into the 21st century, the rapid advancement of artificial intelligence, virtual reality, biotechnology, and other digital innovations will continue to influence every aspect of human life, including relationships, communication, and self-perception. While these advancements bring incredible possibilities, they also present complex ethical and emotional challenges that society must navigate carefully. The way technology integrates with our emotions, decision-making, and daily routines will redefine what it means to be human.

One of the most profound ways technology will continue to shape us is through artificial intelligence. AI is already embedded in our daily lives, from recommendation algorithms on streaming services to personalized search results and virtual assistants like Siri and Alexa. In the future, AI will become even more sophisticated, acting as personal life coaches, decision-making aides, and even emotional support companions. AI-driven mental health apps will provide real-time emotional analysis, detecting stress levels and offering coping strategies tailored to an individual's behavior. While these innovations will improve well-being and self-awareness, they also raise concerns about over-reliance on technology and the potential for AI to manipulate emotions or reinforce biases.

Virtual and augmented reality will further blur the lines between the physical and digital worlds, redefining how we experience relationships, entertainment, and social interactions. By 2050, immersive VR environments will allow people to engage in hyper-realistic experiences that mimic real-life interactions, from attending concerts to traveling to far-off destinations without leaving their homes. These virtual spaces will enhance global connectivity, enabling people from different parts of the world to form friendships, build relationships, and collaborate on projects as if they were in the same room. However, as virtual experiences become more realistic, concerns about digital addiction, social detachment, and the erosion of in-person interactions will need to be addressed.

Biotechnology and neural interfaces will also play a significant role in shaping the human experience. Brain-computer interfaces (BCIs) will enable direct communication between the mind and machines, allowing individuals to control devices, share thoughts, and even transfer memories through neural connections. This could revolutionize how we learn, communicate, and interact with one another, enhancing empathy and understanding. However, these advancements also raise ethical concerns about privacy, cognitive manipulation, and the potential for misuse by corporations or governments. If thoughts and emotions can be accessed or influenced through technology, maintaining autonomy and personal identity will become critical challenges.

Technology will also redefine our sense of self and identity. Social media, AI-generated content, and digital avatars are already influencing how people perceive themselves and present themselves to the world. In the future, AI-powered personal assistants could curate a digital version of an individual's personality, allowing for virtual presence even after death. The rise of deepfake technology and AI-generated human replicas will challenge authenticity, making it increasingly difficult to distinguish between real and artificial interactions. This will force society to reconsider what it means to be genuine in a world where digital personas can be tailored and manipulated with ease.

Ultimately, technology will continue to shape us in ways we cannot fully predict, offering both extraordinary opportunities and unprecedented ethical dilemmas. The key to navigating this transformation will be maintaining a balance between embracing innovation and preserving our fundamental human values. While technology will enhance convenience, intelligence, and connectivity, it is essential to ensure that it serves humanity rather than replaces the core aspects of human experience—empathy, creativity, and authentic connection. As we continue to evolve alongside technology, the challenge will be to harness its potential while remaining grounded in what makes us truly human.

Embracing Change Without Losing Connection

As the world rapidly evolves through technological advancements, shifting social norms, and global challenges, maintaining meaningful human connections has become both more important and more difficult. While change is inevitable, the challenge lies in embracing innovation without losing the emotional depth and authenticity that define human relationships. As we integrate artificial intelligence, virtual reality, and digital communication into daily life, it is crucial to ensure that these tools enhance rather than replace genuine connections. The key to navigating this transition lies in balancing the benefits of modern advancements with the timeless need for emotional closeness, trust, and shared experiences.

One of the greatest shifts in human interaction has been the rise of digital communication. While instant messaging, social media, and video calls allow people to stay connected across great distances, they have also changed the way we express emotions and form relationships. Digital conversations often lack the nuances of face-to-face interactions, such as body language, tone, and spontaneous moments of connection. In embracing these new forms of communication, it is important to be mindful of maintaining emotional depth by prioritizing meaningful conversations, active listening, and regular in-person interactions whenever possible. Technology should act as a bridge, not a substitute, for real human relationships.

Another significant challenge in the modern world is the increasing reliance on artificial intelligence in social interactions. AI-driven companionship, whether in the form of chatbots, virtual assistants, or even humanoid robots, is becoming more common. While these technologies can provide support, reduce loneliness, and offer entertainment, they cannot replace the emotional complexity of human relationships. AI lacks true empathy, unpredictability, and shared personal history—elements that are fundamental to genuine connection. To embrace change without losing our ability to connect, people must ensure that AI remains a tool to enhance relationships rather than a replacement for real emotional intimacy.

The rise of remote work and digital lifestyles has also affected how people maintain relationships. With fewer daily face-to-face interactions, both professional and personal relationships can suffer from a lack of spontaneity and emotional engagement. While digital tools make collaboration and communication easier, they do not fully replicate the social bonds formed in physical spaces. To counteract this, individuals and communities must actively create opportunities for real-world interactions—whether through social gatherings, shared activities, or intentional time spent together. Maintaining strong relationships in a digital age requires effort and mindfulness, ensuring that convenience does not come at the cost of genuine connection.

As society embraces change, the most important factor in maintaining connection is intentionality. Love, friendship, and family bonds thrive not just on convenience but on effort, presence, and shared experiences. It is essential to balance the benefits of modern tools with the irreplaceable value of in-person interactions, deep conversations, and emotional vulnerability. By using technology as a means to strengthen rather than replace relationships, people can embrace progress while holding onto what makes human connection truly meaningful. In a world of rapid transformation, the ability to adapt while prioritizing real, heartfelt connections will be the foundation of lasting relationships and emotional fulfillment.

Cahpter 10
A Timeless Tale

As the world rapidly evolves through technological advancements, shifting social norms, and global challenges, maintaining meaningful human connections has become both more important and more difficult. While change is inevitable, the challenge lies in embracing innovation without losing the emotional depth and authenticity that define human relationships. As we integrate artificial intelligence, virtual reality, and digital communication into daily life, it is crucial to ensure that these tools enhance rather than replace genuine connections. The key to navigating this transition lies in balancing the benefits of modern advancements with the timeless need for emotional closeness, trust, and shared experiences.

One of the greatest shifts in human interaction has been the rise of digital communication. While instant messaging, social media, and video calls allow people to stay connected across great distances, they have also changed the way we express emotions and form relationships. Digital conversations often lack the nuances of face-to-face interactions, such as body language, tone, and spontaneous moments of connection. In embracing these new forms of communication, it is important to be mindful of maintaining emotional depth by prioritizing meaningful conversations, active listening, and regular in-person interactions whenever possible. Technology should act as a bridge, not a substitute, for real human relationships.

Another significant challenge in the modern world is the increasing reliance on artificial intelligence in social interactions. AI-driven companionship, whether in the form of chatbots, virtual assistants, or even humanoid robots, is becoming more common. While these technologies can provide support, reduce loneliness, and offer entertainment, they cannot replace the emotional complexity of human relationships. AI lacks true empathy, unpredictability, and shared personal history—elements that are fundamental to genuine connection. To embrace change without losing our ability to connect, people must ensure that AI remains a tool to enhance relationships rather than a replacement for real emotional intimacy.

The rise of remote work and digital lifestyles has also affected how people maintain relationships. With fewer daily face-to-face interactions, both professional and personal relationships can suffer from a lack of spontaneity and emotional engagement. While digital tools make collaboration and communication easier, they do not fully replicate the social bonds formed in physical spaces. To counteract this, individuals and communities must actively create opportunities for real-world interactions—whether through social gatherings, shared activities, or intentional time spent together. Maintaining strong relationships in a digital age requires effort and mindfulness, ensuring that convenience does not come at the cost of genuine connection.

As society embraces change, the most important factor in maintaining connection is intentionality. Love, friendship, and family bonds thrive not just on convenience but on effort, presence, and shared experiences. It is essential to balance the benefits of modern tools with the irreplaceable value of in-person interactions, deep conversations, and emotional vulnerability. By using technology as a means to strengthen rather than replace relationships, people can embrace progress while holding onto what makes human connection truly meaningful. In a world of rapid transformation, the ability to adapt while prioritizing real, heartfelt connections will be the foundation of lasting relationships and emotional fulfillment.

Lessons from the Journey

Every journey, whether personal, relational, or societal, brings with it invaluable lessons that shape our understanding of ourselves and the world around us. As love, technology, and human connection continue to evolve, the experiences we gather along the way offer profound insights into resilience, adaptability, and the enduring nature of relationships. The modern world, with its rapid changes and unexpected challenges, has redefined the way people approach love and connection, teaching us that while circumstances may shift, the fundamental human need for understanding, companionship, and emotional security remains unchanged.

One of the most significant lessons from this journey is the importance of adaptability. The world has seen immense transformation, from the rise of digital communication to the integration of artificial intelligence in relationships. These changes have challenged traditional notions of intimacy and dating, pushing people to embrace new ways of connecting. Whether it is long-distance couples relying on virtual reality to feel close or individuals forming deep bonds through online platforms, adaptability has become a crucial skill in navigating modern relationships. Learning to evolve alongside technology while maintaining emotional depth has proven essential in preserving meaningful connections.

Another key lesson is that authenticity matters more than ever. In a world where digital interactions often replace face-to-face communication, the risk of superficiality is high. Social media encourages curated versions of reality, dating apps reduce love to quick swipes, and AI companions offer relationships without emotional complexity. However, the most fulfilling connections come from authenticity—being honest about emotions, embracing imperfections, and prioritizing real conversations over polished appearances. The lesson here is clear: technology should enhance, not replace, genuine human connection. Emotional depth and vulnerability remain the cornerstones of strong, lasting relationships.

The journey also teaches us the value of intentionality. With so many distractions, from the constant notifications of social media to the fast-paced nature of modern life, maintaining deep relationships requires effort. Love does not thrive on autopilot; it demands conscious investment in time, energy, and emotional presence. Whether through heartfelt conversations, shared experiences, or simply being present in the moment, relationships are nurtured through intentional acts of care. Those who prioritize their connections—despite the convenience of digital shortcuts—find that love remains one of the most rewarding aspects of life.

Perhaps the most important lesson is that love, in all its forms, is ever-evolving but never obsolete. While the mediums through which people connect may change, the desire for companionship, understanding, and emotional security is timeless. Whether love is expressed through handwritten letters, video calls, or virtual reality, its essence remains unchanged. The ability to love, to be loved, and to form deep connections is what makes us human. As the world continues to advance, this lesson remains constant: love is not defined by the tools we use but by the sincerity of the emotions we share.

In the end, the journey of love and connection is one of growth, learning, and adaptation. The lessons we gather remind us that while change is inevitable, the core of human relationships—trust, empathy, and emotional depth—will always stand the test of time. By embracing change while staying true to what makes love meaningful, we ensure that no matter how the world evolves, our connections remain strong, genuine, and deeply fulfilling.

Love's Eternal Nature

Despite the ever-changing world, love remains one of the few constants in human existence. Across generations, civilizations, and technological revolutions, love has persisted as an enduring force that transcends time, space, and societal shifts. While the ways in which people express love evolve—moving from handwritten letters to instant messages, from chance meetings to AI-driven matchmaking—the essence of love remains untouched. It is a universal experience, a profound connection that withstands the test of time, proving that no matter how much the world changes, love's eternal nature remains at the heart of the human experience.

One of the reasons love endures is its adaptability. Throughout history, love has found a way to thrive in different circumstances. In times of war, love letters sustained long-distance connections. During periods of societal change, love broke barriers, defied norms, and persisted despite obstacles. In modern times, digital communication has allowed relationships to flourish across continents, proving that love is not confined by physical presence. Even as artificial intelligence and virtual reality reshape interactions, the core of love remains unchanged—people seek understanding, connection, and emotional fulfillment, regardless of the medium through which they find it.

Another testament to love's eternal nature is its deep emotional impact. Love is not just a fleeting emotion; it is a transformative experience that shapes identities, influences decisions, and creates lasting memories. From the first moments of infatuation to lifelong partnerships built on trust and commitment, love leaves an indelible mark on those who experience it. It teaches patience, resilience, and selflessness, reinforcing the idea that love is not merely a feeling but a journey—one that evolves with time but never loses its significance.

Love also persists because it is deeply embedded in human nature. Scientific studies have shown that love is not just an abstract concept but a fundamental part of human survival. From the bonds between parents and children to romantic partnerships and friendships, love provides emotional security, promotes well-being, and fosters cooperation. It is what drives people to care for one another, to build families, and to seek companionship even in the most challenging circumstances. Regardless of technological advancements or cultural transformations, the human need for love remains unchanged, proving its eternal presence in our lives.

Even in the face of loss, love continues to exist. The memory of love, the impact of a cherished relationship, and the lessons learned from a deep connection do not fade with time. Love transcends physical presence, living on in stories, traditions, and the hearts of those who carry it forward. It is why people honor the love of those who have passed, why they hold onto moments of love long after they have ended, and why they continue to seek it despite past heartbreaks. Love is not bound by time or circumstance—it endures, it heals, and it inspires.

Ultimately, love's eternal nature is a testament to its power. While the world continues to evolve, love remains unshaken, proving that it is not defined by changing trends, new technologies, or societal expectations. Love is timeless, resilient, and infinite. It is the force that connects humanity across generations, reminding us that no matter where we are in history, love will always be a guiding light in the human experience.

Writing Your Own Modern Valentine's Tale

Love stories have always been a part of human history, evolving with time to reflect the changing landscapes of relationships, technology, and cultural values. In the modern era, where digital communication, virtual reality, and artificial intelligence influence romance, writing your own modern Valentine's tale is both an exciting and deeply personal journey. Unlike the grand romantic gestures of classic literature, today's love stories are shaped by unique experiences, meaningful conversations, and connections that transcend physical boundaries. Whether you are in a long-distance relationship, navigating love through dating apps, or embracing non-traditional partnerships, your love story is yours to create, celebrate, and cherish.

A modern Valentine's tale often begins with an unconventional meeting. Gone are the days when romance was strictly confined to chance encounters at coffee shops or letters exchanged over months. Today, love can spark from a simple swipe on a dating app, a shared interest in an online community, or even a conversation in a virtual reality world. The rise of technology has expanded the ways in which people connect, proving that love is no longer limited by geography or traditional social settings. However, what makes a love story meaningful is not how two people meet but how they grow together, navigate challenges, and build a relationship that withstands the test of time.

One of the defining aspects of a modern love story is the role of communication. In a world where instant messaging, video calls, and social media dominate interactions, expressing love has taken on new dimensions. While digital tools make it easier to stay in touch, they also require effort to maintain emotional depth. Writing your own Valentine's tale means prioritizing heartfelt conversations, finding creative ways to show appreciation, and ensuring that technology enhances, rather than replaces, genuine intimacy. Whether it's a long-distance relationship where partners write digital love letters or a couple that bonds over shared playlists and late-night calls, modern romance thrives on intentional communication.

Every love story has its challenges, and in today's fast-paced world, balancing personal ambitions, social expectations, and relationship dynamics can be difficult. A modern Valentine's tale is not about perfection but about resilience, growth, and the willingness to navigate life's complexities together. Unlike fairy-tale romances, real love requires understanding, compromise, and a commitment to evolving as individuals while strengthening the relationship. Whether it's overcoming the barriers of distance, adapting to different love languages, or learning to communicate effectively, modern love is built on the ability to face obstacles as a team.

Ultimately, writing your own modern Valentine's tale means defining love on your own terms. It's about embracing the moments—big and small—that make your relationship unique. Whether that means planning a virtual date under the stars, exchanging handwritten notes in a world of texts, or simply being present for each other in meaningful ways, love is about the connection you nurture. Your love story does not have to follow traditional paths or societal expectations—it is yours to shape, celebrate, and cherish. In the end, the most beautiful modern love stories are not defined by technology or trends but by the depth of the emotions shared between two people.

Chapter 11
The Digital Cupid

In the modern era, matchmaking has evolved from handwritten love letters and chance encounters to complex algorithms and artificial intelligence. The traditional Cupid, once depicted with a bow and arrow, has now been replaced by data-driven matchmaking tools, dating apps, and AI-powered compatibility tests. This transformation has made it easier than ever to find a potential partner, with digital platforms analyzing interests, behaviors, and preferences to create seemingly perfect matches. The rise of the "Digital Cupid" represents a shift in how people approach love, favoring efficiency, compatibility, and science over fate and serendipity.

Despite the convenience that digital matchmaking offers, it also comes with its own set of challenges. The abundance of choices on dating apps can lead to decision fatigue, making it difficult for individuals to commit when endless possibilities are just a swipe away. Additionally, algorithms, while powerful, are not perfect—they may prioritize surface-level similarities rather than deeper emotional connections. The risk of misrepresentation also increases in a digital-first dating culture, where profiles are carefully curated and interactions lack the nuances of face-to-face chemistry. While the Digital Cupid can introduce two compatible individuals, the success of a relationship still depends on real-world interactions, emotional intelligence, and shared experiences.

Yet, there is no denying that technology has revolutionized modern love, bridging gaps that once seemed insurmountable. Long-distance relationships are now sustained through instant messaging and video calls, while virtual reality and artificial intelligence are redefining intimacy in new and exciting ways. For better or worse, the Digital Cupid is here to stay, continuously evolving to refine the way people find and experience love. As society embraces these changes, the challenge lies in using technology to enhance human connection rather than replace it, ensuring that love remains a deeply personal and meaningful experience.

The Evolution of Matchmaking

Matchmaking has been a fundamental part of human relationships for centuries, evolving from traditional, community-based practices to sophisticated digital algorithms that shape modern dating. The way people find love has changed dramatically over time, influenced by cultural shifts, technological advancements, and societal expectations. While the desire for companionship has remained constant, the methods used to connect individuals have continuously adapted to the world around them. From arranged marriages and handwritten love letters to dating apps and AI-driven compatibility assessments, the evolution of matchmaking reflects humanity's enduring quest for meaningful connections.

Historically, matchmaking was a communal effort, often guided by family members, religious leaders, or professional matchmakers. In many cultures, marriages were arranged to ensure social, economic, or political stability rather than romantic compatibility. Love was often expected to grow within the marriage rather than serve as its foundation. Courtship rituals varied across societies, with some relying on family negotiations while others placed importance on social events and formal introductions. During the Victorian era, for example, courtship was a structured process where letters, chaperoned meetings, and public outings were the primary means of romantic interaction. These methods, while restrictive by modern standards, reflected the values and traditions of their time.

As industrialization and urbanization transformed societies, matchmaking became more independent and personal. The 20th century saw the rise of personal ads in newspapers, where individuals would describe themselves and the type of partner they were seeking. By the mid-century, matchmaking agencies and dating services emerged, offering a more structured approach to finding love. Speed dating, video dating, and singles events gained popularity, allowing people to meet potential partners in controlled environments. The introduction of computers in the 1960s even led to early forms of digital matchmaking, with some services using questionnaires to pair compatible individuals based on personality traits and shared interests.

The digital age brought the most significant revolution in matchmaking, shifting the process from in-person introductions to online interactions. The launch of online dating sites in the 1990s and early 2000s, such as Match.com and eHarmony, allowed people to create profiles and search for potential partners using filters and algorithms. Dating apps, like Tinder, revolutionized matchmaking by making it instant, mobile, and widely accessible. Swiping culture introduced an entirely new way to engage with potential partners, emphasizing first impressions and immediate attraction. While this increased convenience and expanded dating pools, it also introduced challenges such as decision fatigue, ghosting, and the paradox of choice—where too many options make commitment difficult.

The latest phase in matchmaking involves artificial intelligence, big data, and even virtual reality. AI-driven dating platforms now analyze vast amounts of data to predict compatibility, offering personalized suggestions rather than random matches. Some dating services incorporate machine learning to refine matches over time, adapting to user preferences and behaviors. Virtual reality is also being explored as a way to create immersive dating experiences, allowing individuals to meet and interact in digital environments before committing to real-life interactions.

Despite these technological advancements, the core principles of matchmaking remain unchanged—people still seek connection, compatibility, and emotional fulfillment. While technology can facilitate introductions, successful relationships continue to rely on trust, communication, and shared experiences. As matchmaking evolves further, the challenge will be to balance efficiency with authenticity, ensuring that love remains a deeply human experience rather than a purely algorithmic outcome.

Algorithms of Attraction

In the digital age, romance is no longer left entirely to fate or chance encounters. Instead, algorithms of attraction have become the invisible matchmakers behind millions of modern relationships, shaping who we meet, who we date, and even who we fall in love with. Dating apps and online matchmaking platforms use complex algorithms to analyze personal data, interests, behaviors, and preferences to suggest potential romantic partners. While these digital formulas have revolutionized the dating landscape, they also raise intriguing questions about the science of compatibility, the role of technology in human emotions, and whether love can truly be reduced to data points.

At the heart of modern matchmaking algorithms is the concept of compatibility scoring. Dating platforms like Tinder, Bumble, and OkCupid use AI-driven formulas that analyze user interactions, swipes, and messaging habits to predict potential romantic matches. Some services go beyond basic preferences and use psychological and behavioral assessments to pair individuals based on deeper compatibility metrics, such as shared values, emotional intelligence, and lifestyle choices. Machine learning allows these platforms to refine recommendations over time, adapting to a user's evolving preferences and improving the quality of matches. By leveraging data science, dating algorithms aim to take the guesswork out of finding a compatible partner, making modern dating both efficient and highly personalized.

However, while algorithms provide a structured way to identify potential matches, they do not guarantee romantic success. Love is complex, unpredictable, and deeply personal—qualities that cannot always be measured by a mathematical formula. Attraction is influenced by subtle, intangible factors such as chemistry, voice tone, body language, and emotional connection, which algorithms cannot fully capture. This limitation often leads to the paradox of choice, where individuals are presented with an overwhelming number of potential matches but struggle to commit due to the perception that someone "better" may be just another swipe away. The efficiency of dating algorithms, while impressive, does not eliminate the human element of trial and error in relationships.

Another concern surrounding attraction algorithms is the possibility of bias. Many dating platforms rely on user-provided data, which can sometimes reinforce stereotypes or create echo chambers of similarity. If an algorithm prioritizes matches based on pre-existing preferences, it may unintentionally limit exposure to diverse dating experiences. This can lead to reinforcing narrow dating patterns rather than encouraging users to explore connections outside their usual comfort zones. Ethical concerns about data privacy also arise, as these platforms collect vast amounts of personal information, raising questions about how such data is used and whether it could be exploited for commercial purposes beyond matchmaking.

Despite these challenges, algorithms of attraction have undeniably reshaped the way people connect in the modern world. They provide access to broader dating pools, create opportunities for meaningful relationships, and leverage technology to enhance human connection. However, while these digital matchmakers can suggest compatibility, they cannot replace the fundamental aspects of building a relationship—trust, emotional depth, and shared experiences. Ultimately, love may begin with an algorithm, but it thrives through the choices, efforts, and emotions of the individuals involved. The future of attraction will likely continue to blend data-driven insights with human intuition, proving that while technology can facilitate romance, the true magic of love still lies beyond the code.

Love in the Age of Swipes

In the era of digital romance, love has become just a swipe away. Dating apps like Tinder, Bumble, Hinge, and OkCupid have transformed the way people meet and form relationships, replacing traditional courtship with quick decisions based on profile pictures, bios, and short conversations. While these platforms offer unprecedented convenience and accessibility, they also introduce new challenges, including superficiality, commitment fatigue, and the paradox of choice. Love in the age of swipes is a reflection of the fast-paced digital world—one where technology facilitates connections, but true intimacy still requires effort, patience, and emotional depth.

The rise of swipe-based dating has fundamentally changed the way people approach attraction and compatibility. Traditional dating relied on in-person chemistry, shared experiences, and gradual emotional development. In contrast, modern dating apps encourage instant judgment based on appearances and minimal profile information. This gamification of love—where users swipe left to reject and right to express interest—has created a dynamic where first impressions carry more weight than deeper compatibility. While this approach increases efficiency by allowing users to browse multiple potential partners in minutes, it also fosters a culture of disposable relationships, where the next option is always just a swipe away.

One of the biggest challenges of love in the age of swipes is the paradox of choice. With an endless stream of potential matches, many individuals struggle to commit, fearing that a better option might be just around the corner. This abundance of choices can lead to decision fatigue, making people more likely to engage in short-term interactions rather than investing in long-term connections. Ghosting, breadcrumbing, and casual encounters have become common side effects of swipe culture, as people cycle through relationships without fully engaging in emotional intimacy. This can create feelings of frustration, loneliness, and detachment, as the pursuit of love becomes an endless loop of swiping rather than a meaningful journey toward companionship.

However, despite these challenges, dating apps have also created opportunities for love that would have been impossible in the past. Long-distance relationships are more viable, introverts and busy professionals can connect with potential partners in ways that fit their lifestyles, and individuals from different backgrounds have the chance to meet in ways that transcend traditional social circles. Many successful relationships and marriages have emerged from swipe-based dating, proving that while the process has changed, the potential for deep and lasting connections remains.

Navigating love in the digital age requires a balance between efficiency and intentionality. While dating apps provide valuable tools for meeting new people, true connection still depends on emotional effort, vulnerability, and shared values. Instead of relying solely on algorithms and first impressions, individuals seeking meaningful relationships must engage in deeper conversations, set clear intentions, and approach dating with a mindset that prioritizes quality over quantity. Love in the age of swipes is not about rejecting technology but learning to use it as a bridge to genuine human connection rather than a barrier to intimacy. In a world where swiping has become the norm, those who approach digital romance with authenticity, patience, and emotional depth will ultimately find the most rewarding relationships.

Chapter 12
Love in the Age of Algorithms

In today's digital world, romance is no longer just about chance encounters, shared interests, or the mysterious pull of chemistry. Instead, love has been transformed by the power of algorithms—data-driven formulas designed to predict compatibility, analyze attraction, and facilitate connections. Dating apps and online matchmaking services now play the role of modern Cupids, using artificial intelligence and behavioral analytics to pair individuals based on personality traits, preferences, and past interactions. While these advancements have made finding potential partners more efficient, they also raise questions about whether love can truly be reduced to data points and mathematical probabilities.

The increasing reliance on technology in dating has reshaped the way people perceive and pursue relationships. Swiping through profiles, engaging in algorithmically suggested conversations, and refining matches based on digital behaviors have created a new landscape for modern romance. While some argue that algorithms help filter out incompatible matches and increase the chances of meaningful relationships, others worry that the process has become too mechanical, stripping away the spontaneity and magic that define human connection. The idea that a computer program can determine emotional compatibility challenges traditional notions of love, which have long been seen as unpredictable and deeply personal.

As love continues to evolve in the digital age, it is essential to explore both the benefits and the limitations of algorithm-driven matchmaking. Can technology truly enhance human relationships, or does it create unrealistic expectations? Are people becoming too reliant on data to dictate their romantic decisions? This chapter delves into the impact of algorithms on modern love, examining how they shape relationships, influence dating culture, and redefine what it means to find "the one" in an age where technology and emotion are increasingly intertwined.

Data-Driven Romance

In the digital age, love is no longer left solely to fate or spontaneous encounters. Instead, romance has become a carefully analyzed equation, driven by data and algorithms designed to predict compatibility. Dating apps, social media platforms, and artificial intelligence now play a significant role in shaping modern relationships, using vast amounts of data to pair individuals based on personality traits, interests, behaviors, and preferences. This shift has transformed the dating landscape, making the process of finding love more efficient, but also raising questions about the role of technology in human connection.

At the heart of data-driven romance is the concept of algorithmic matchmaking. Dating platforms like Tinder, Hinge, OkCupid, and eHarmony rely on complex formulas to suggest potential partners based on user behavior. These algorithms analyze everything from the way a person swipes and how long they spend on a profile to shared interests, location, and past conversations. Some platforms even incorporate artificial intelligence to refine matches over time, adapting to users' evolving preferences. This level of personalization aims to increase the likelihood of finding a compatible partner by filtering out individuals who may not align with one's values, lifestyle, or long-term goals.

While data-driven romance offers efficiency and convenience, it also introduces challenges. One major concern is whether algorithms can truly capture the depth and complexity of human attraction. Love is influenced by subtle, unpredictable factors—body language, humor, chemistry—that cannot always be quantified by data points. While digital platforms can suggest potential matches, they cannot guarantee emotional compatibility or genuine connection. This reliance on technology has also led to the paradox of choice, where users are overwhelmed by an abundance of potential partners, making it difficult to commit or invest deeply in a single relationship. The ease of swiping to find someone new often leads to a culture of disposable dating, where connections are abandoned at the first sign of imperfection.

Another significant aspect of data-driven romance is the ethical concern surrounding privacy and manipulation. Dating apps collect vast amounts of personal data, raising questions about how this information is stored, used, and potentially monetized. Some platforms use engagement metrics to keep users swiping rather than genuinely helping them find a match, prioritizing prolonged app usage over meaningful connections. Additionally, algorithms may reinforce biases, limiting the diversity of matches by prioritizing individuals who fit specific patterns of attraction. This can create echo chambers where users are repeatedly exposed to similar profiles, reducing the opportunity for unexpected and meaningful encounters.

Despite these challenges, data-driven romance has undeniably reshaped the way people meet and form relationships. Many couples who met through dating apps have built successful, long-term partnerships, proving that technology can play a valuable role in modern love. However, true connection still requires effort beyond the algorithm. While data can help facilitate introductions, meaningful relationships are built through emotional depth, shared experiences, and authentic communication. In the end, love may begin with an algorithm, but it thrives through human interaction, proving that while technology can guide romance, it cannot replace the essence of real connection.

AI and Emotional Intelligence

Artificial intelligence (AI) has made significant advancements in understanding human emotions, revolutionizing the way people interact with technology and each other. From AI-powered chatbots offering emotional support to dating algorithms that assess compatibility based on personality traits, AI is increasingly influencing the emotional landscape of human relationships. However, while AI can analyze, predict, and even mimic emotions, the question remains: can AI truly possess emotional intelligence, or is it simply replicating human behavior based on data and patterns? As AI continues to evolve, its role in emotional interactions raises complex ethical, psychological, and philosophical questions about the nature of genuine connection.

One of the most promising aspects of AI's relationship with emotional intelligence is its ability to recognize and respond to human emotions. Machine learning models and natural language processing have allowed AI systems to analyze tone, sentiment, and facial expressions to gauge emotional states. AI-driven mental health chatbots, such as Woebot and Replika, have been designed to provide emotional support by engaging in conversations that help users express their feelings and navigate stress or anxiety. Virtual assistants like Alexa and Google Assistant are also being enhanced with emotion-detection capabilities to make interactions more human-like. While these AI tools can offer companionship and comfort, they lack the intrinsic empathy and consciousness that define genuine human emotional intelligence.

AI's ability to process vast amounts of data also enables it to predict emotional responses and personalize interactions in ways that humans cannot. Dating apps, for instance, use AI to analyze users' past interactions, preferences, and even the language they use in messages to suggest more compatible matches. Some AI systems are even being developed to provide relationship advice, analyzing communication patterns between partners to identify potential conflicts and suggest ways to improve understanding. While these advancements can enhance human relationships, they also raise concerns about whether people will become too reliant on AI for emotional validation rather than developing their own emotional intelligence through real-life experiences.

Despite AI's ability to simulate emotions, its limitations in true emotional intelligence become evident in complex social interactions. Emotional intelligence in humans is shaped by personal experiences, cultural backgrounds, and an intuitive understanding of social dynamics—elements that AI lacks. While AI can recognize sadness in a person's voice and offer comforting words, it does not truly "feel" compassion, nor does it experience emotions firsthand. This absence of genuine emotional depth makes it difficult for AI to navigate moral dilemmas, nuanced interpersonal relationships, and the unpredictability of human emotions. AI's responses, no matter how advanced, are still based on pre-programmed logic and learned data rather than genuine sentiment.

As AI becomes more integrated into human relationships, it is crucial to recognize the distinction between AI's ability to process emotions and the human capacity to truly feel them. AI can enhance emotional interactions by offering support, predicting compatibility, and improving communication, but it cannot replace the depth, spontaneity, and authenticity of human connection. The future of AI in emotional intelligence will depend on how well society balances technological advancements with the irreplaceable qualities of human empathy, intuition, and genuine emotional depth.

The Science of Compatibility

Compatibility has long been a central factor in successful relationships, but in today's data-driven world, it is increasingly being studied, measured, and analyzed through science. Researchers, psychologists, and artificial intelligence experts have sought to understand what makes two people compatible, breaking love down into psychological traits, biological factors, and behavioral patterns. Whether through personality assessments, genetic studies, or algorithm-driven matchmaking, the science of compatibility attempts to predict and optimize romantic relationships. However, while science can provide valuable insights, it cannot fully account for the unpredictability, chemistry, and emotional depth that define human connection.

One of the most widely used approaches in compatibility science is psychological profiling. Many dating platforms and matchmaking services utilize personality assessments based on psychological theories, such as the Big Five Personality Traits (openness, conscientiousness, extraversion, agreeableness, and neuroticism). Research suggests that individuals with complementary or balanced personality traits are more likely to form stable and fulfilling relationships. For example, a highly extroverted person may benefit from a partner with a more calming influence, while two highly conscientious individuals may build a strong partnership based on mutual organization and reliability. While these assessments can provide useful indicators, they do not guarantee romantic success, as human relationships are influenced by factors beyond personality compatibility, such as emotional intelligence, communication skills, and life circumstances.

Biological compatibility has also been explored as a key determinant of attraction and relationship success. Studies suggest that factors like genetics and pheromones play a role in attraction, with some researchers arguing that individuals are subconsciously drawn to partners with different immune system genes (Major Histocompatibility Complex, or MHC) to promote genetic diversity in offspring. Other studies have examined the role of brain chemistry in love, revealing that neurotransmitters like dopamine, oxytocin, and serotonin influence attraction, bonding, and long-term attachment. While these biological factors may play a role in initial attraction, they are not sufficient to predict long-term relationship success, as relationships require emotional connection, shared values, and mutual effort to thrive.

In recent years, artificial intelligence and big data have been incorporated into compatibility science, using machine learning to analyze massive amounts of relationship data. Dating apps and matchmaking services now use behavioral analytics to refine matches based on user preferences, past interactions, and success rates of similar couples. These platforms claim to increase compatibility by considering shared interests, lifestyle choices, and communication styles. However, the reliance on data-driven compatibility raises concerns about reducing love to an algorithm. Chemistry, spontaneity, and emotional depth cannot be fully captured by an AI system, making it important for individuals to approach matchmaking tools as aids rather than definitive predictors of love.

Ultimately, while science offers fascinating insights into compatibility, relationships remain deeply personal and dynamic experiences. Attraction, love, and long-term success involve a combination of psychological, biological, and emotional factors, many of which cannot be quantified or predicted. True compatibility is not just about matching scores or genetic markers—it is about shared experiences, trust, emotional support, and a willingness to grow together. Science may help guide individuals toward better matches, but the true essence of love remains uniquely human, shaped by the unpredictable and beautiful complexities of real-life relationships.

Chapter.13
Swiping for Soulmates

In the modern age of digital dating, the search for a soulmate has been transformed by the simple act of swiping. With the rise of dating apps like Tinder, Bumble, and Hinge, love is now just a screen tap away, allowing individuals to browse through countless profiles in search of the perfect match. This gamification of romance has revolutionized how people meet and connect, offering convenience, efficiency, and access to a larger dating pool than ever before. However, while swiping provides new opportunities for love, it also raises questions about the depth of modern relationships and whether technology can truly help people find their soulmates.

Swiping-based dating has redefined attraction by prioritizing first impressions and instant judgments. Unlike traditional courtship, which allows chemistry to develop gradually, digital dating platforms encourage quick decisions based on profile pictures and brief bios. While this approach makes it easier to filter through potential partners, it can also lead to a culture of superficiality, where physical appearance is often the determining factor. The sheer abundance of options can also create the paradox of choice—where having too many possibilities makes it harder to commit, as users are constantly tempted by the idea that someone better may be just one swipe away.

Despite its challenges, swiping has led to many successful relationships and even marriages, proving that digital matchmaking can be effective when approached with the right mindset. Many individuals have found meaningful connections through dating apps, demonstrating that technology can facilitate deep relationships when used with intention and authenticity. This chapter explores the evolution of swiping culture, the psychology behind digital attraction, and strategies for navigating the digital dating landscape in the search for true love.

The Psychology of Dating Apps

Dating apps have revolutionized modern romance, transforming the way people meet, form connections, and pursue relationships. While these platforms provide convenience, accessibility, and a seemingly endless pool of potential matches, they also influence human psychology in profound ways. From the mechanics of swiping to the emotional highs and lows of online dating, the psychology behind dating apps affects behavior, self-esteem, and relationship expectations. Understanding the psychological factors at play can help individuals navigate the digital dating landscape more effectively, making more intentional choices in their search for meaningful connections.

One of the most significant psychological mechanisms driving dating apps is **the gamification of attraction**. Platforms like Tinder, Bumble, and Hinge have turned dating into an interactive experience that closely resembles a game. The simple action of swiping left to reject or right to express interest triggers a dopamine response in the brain, similar to the satisfaction experienced in gaming or social media engagement. Each match or positive interaction provides a rush of excitement, reinforcing the habit of swiping. This reward-based system keeps users engaged, sometimes more for the thrill of matching than for actually pursuing a relationship. While this design increases user retention on dating apps, it can also lead to addictive behaviors, where people prioritize the act of swiping over building real connections.

Another key psychological factor in dating apps is **the paradox of choice**. In traditional dating, individuals typically meet a limited number of potential partners through work, social circles, or chance encounters. Dating apps, however, present an overwhelming number of options, which can lead to decision fatigue. When faced with too many choices, individuals may struggle to commit, always wondering if a better match is just another swipe away. This phenomenon can result in a pattern of short-lived conversations, ghosting, and a reluctance to invest in a single relationship. The abundance of options may give the illusion of infinite opportunities but can also prevent users from forming deep, meaningful connections.

Self-presentation and **the psychology of online attraction** also play a crucial role in digital dating. Because dating profiles are often a person's first impression, individuals tend to curate their images and bios to highlight their most attractive traits. This leads to the phenomenon of **profile optimization**, where users carefully select photos, craft witty descriptions, and even edit or exaggerate certain aspects of their lives to appeal to potential matches. While this behavior is natural in any dating context, the gap between online personas and real-life personalities can sometimes lead to disappointment. Studies have shown that mismatches between online expectations and in-person reality contribute to the high rate of short-lived connections formed through dating apps.

Despite these psychological challenges, dating apps can be valuable tools for meeting like-minded individuals when used with the right mindset. Being aware of the potential pitfalls—such as addictive swiping behaviors, unrealistic expectations, and decision fatigue—allows users to approach digital dating with more intentionality. By prioritizing meaningful conversations, setting realistic expectations, and taking breaks from the app when needed, individuals can harness the power of technology while maintaining emotional well-being. Ultimately, while dating apps influence human psychology in complex ways, they remain tools that, when used mindfully, can lead to genuine and lasting relationships.

From Text to Connection

In the age of digital dating, relationships often begin with a simple text. Whether it's a swipe-right match on a dating app or a message on social media, modern romance frequently starts with a conversation in a virtual space before transitioning into real-world interactions. However, turning an exchange of texts into a meaningful connection requires more than just witty responses and emojis. Building intimacy through digital communication presents unique challenges and opportunities, shaping the way people form emotional bonds in a world where texting has become the first step toward love.

One of the key aspects of forming a connection through text is **effective communication**. Unlike face-to-face interactions, where body language, tone, and facial expressions convey emotions, texting relies solely on words. This limitation makes it easy for messages to be misinterpreted, leading to confusion or even unintended conflicts. Without the nuances of spoken conversation, humor can fall flat, sarcasm can be misread, and emotional intent can be unclear. To bridge this gap, people often use emojis, GIFs, and punctuation to add context to their messages. While these tools help, they still require both parties to engage actively and interpret communication with patience and emotional intelligence. Successful digital interactions often stem from thoughtful messaging, where both individuals take the time to understand and respond meaningfully rather than relying on short, surface-level exchanges.

Another crucial factor in moving from text to connection is **emotional investment**. Texting can be a powerful tool for building anticipation, allowing people to share thoughts, stories, and even vulnerabilities before meeting in person. When conversations go beyond small talk—diving into personal interests, future goals, and meaningful experiences—texting can foster a sense of emotional intimacy. However, this stage can also create a false sense of connection if not balanced with real-world experiences. It's easy to project fantasies onto a person we've never met, imagining a relationship based on words rather than actual chemistry. This is why prolonged digital-only interactions can sometimes lead to disappointment when the transition to in-person meetings doesn't align with the emotional depth built over text.

The ultimate challenge in transforming texting into a real connection is bridging the gap between digital and physical interactions. While messaging is a convenient way to get to know someone, true intimacy is formed through shared experiences, in-person chemistry, and non-verbal communication. Many digital relationships fizzle out because they remain confined to text without progressing into real-world interactions. To overcome this, both individuals must show willingness to move beyond the screen—whether through phone calls, video chats, or in-person meetings. A successful transition from text to connection requires effort from both sides, ensuring that digital communication serves as a stepping stone rather than a substitute for genuine interaction.

In the modern dating landscape, texting is an essential part of relationship-building, but it should not replace real emotional bonding. While technology allows people to connect across distances and start relationships in new ways, the key to lasting intimacy lies in transitioning from digital conversations to meaningful, real-life connections. By prioritizing open communication, emotional authenticity, and a proactive approach to meeting in person, individuals can turn text-based interactions into relationships that thrive beyond the screen.

Navigating the Digital Dating Scene

The digital dating scene has revolutionized the way people connect, making it easier than ever to meet potential partners with just a few swipes or clicks. However, while technology has expanded the dating pool and increased accessibility, it has also introduced new challenges that require a thoughtful and strategic approach. Navigating online dating successfully involves understanding the dynamics of digital attraction, avoiding common pitfalls, and prioritizing meaningful connections over fleeting interactions. As the landscape of modern romance continues to evolve, learning how to engage effectively in the digital dating world can lead to more fulfilling and authentic relationships.

One of the first challenges of digital dating is creating an authentic and appealing profile. First impressions happen in an instant, and on dating apps, they are often based solely on a handful of pictures and a short bio. Striking a balance between showcasing personality and maintaining authenticity is crucial. Many people fall into the trap of overly curating their profiles, selecting only highly edited or outdated photos and crafting bios that may not fully represent who they are. While making a strong first impression is important, honesty remains the key to attracting like-minded individuals. A well-crafted profile should highlight personal interests, values, and a sense of humor while remaining genuine and relatable. Transparency about relationship intentions—whether casual dating or serious commitment—also helps filter out mismatched connections early on.

Another essential aspect of digital dating is learning how to communicate effectively. Unlike traditional dating, where chemistry is felt in person, online interactions depend on messages, emojis, and video calls. This format presents both opportunities and challenges. Engaging conversations require more than just basic greetings or generic openers—personalized messages that reference something from the other person's profile create better engagement and demonstrate genuine interest. However, digital communication can sometimes lead to misunderstandings, as text messages lack the nuances of tone and body language. Overcoming this requires patience, clarity, and, when possible, transitioning to phone or video calls to establish a deeper connection.

One of the most common struggles in the digital dating scene is handling the abundance of choices and avoiding dating fatigue. With an endless stream of profiles available, many users experience the paradox of choice—where having too many options makes it harder to commit. This can lead to a cycle of swiping without meaningful engagement, causing dating to feel like a numbers game rather than a path to genuine relationships. Additionally, frequent exposure to online rejection, ghosting, or superficial conversations can lead to dating burnout. To prevent this, it's important to set realistic expectations, take breaks when needed, and focus on quality over quantity. Instead of swiping endlessly, engaging meaningfully with a few potential matches can lead to more substantial and rewarding connections.

Ultimately, navigating the digital dating scene requires a balance of optimism, patience, and self-awareness. While technology has changed how people meet, the fundamentals of successful relationships—honest communication, emotional depth, and shared values—remain the same. By approaching digital dating with intentionality, staying true to oneself, and prioritizing real connections over superficial interactions, individuals can turn online encounters into meaningful, lasting relationships.

Chapter 14
The Promise of Perfect Matches

In the digital age, the search for love has been transformed by sophisticated algorithms and AI-driven matchmaking tools that promise to find the perfect partner. Dating apps and online platforms claim to use science, psychology, and big data to analyze compatibility, offering users curated matches that align with their personalities, values, and romantic preferences. This technological approach to romance has created a sense of optimism among those seeking love, as it suggests that finding a soulmate is no longer just a matter of chance but a result of precise calculations and compatibility scores. The promise of perfect matches has made modern dating more efficient, structured, and accessible to people from all walks of life.

However, despite the scientific advancements behind digital matchmaking, love remains an unpredictable and deeply personal experience. While algorithms can suggest partners based on shared interests and psychological traits, they cannot account for the intangible aspects of human connection—chemistry, emotional resonance, and the spontaneity of attraction. Many individuals find that even highly compatible matches on paper do not always translate into real-world romance. This raises the question: can technology truly deliver perfect matches, or is love still an unpredictable journey that defies calculation?

This chapter explores the promise and limitations of algorithm-driven romance, examining whether technology can genuinely create ideal partnerships or if it simply facilitates introductions. While AI and data-driven matchmaking have undoubtedly revolutionized the dating landscape, meaningful relationships still require emotional effort, communication, and mutual growth. Understanding the balance between science and human experience is essential in determining whether perfect matches are a reality or simply a hopeful illusion in the ever-evolving world of love and relationships.

The Illusion of Choice

In the digital dating world, the promise of endless possibilities creates an illusion of unlimited choice. With thousands of potential matches just a swipe away, dating apps give the impression that the perfect partner is always within reach. While this abundance of options seems empowering, it often leads to decision paralysis, unrealistic expectations, and difficulty committing to a single relationship. The illusion of choice, rather than making love easier to find, can sometimes make it harder, as individuals struggle with the paradox of whether to settle for a good match or keep searching for an even better one.

One of the key challenges created by this illusion is decision fatigue. When presented with too many options, people tend to feel overwhelmed, making it difficult to make a confident choice. In traditional dating, where potential partners were met through social circles or chance encounters, individuals focused on nurturing the connections available to them. In contrast, dating apps encourage rapid decision-making, with users often swiping based on superficial first impressions. This creates a mindset where potential partners are easily dismissed in favor of finding someone "better," leading to an endless cycle of swiping rather than meaningful engagement. The more choices people have, the harder it becomes to commit to any one person, as the fear of missing out (FOMO) keeps them searching for the elusive "perfect" match.

Another consequence of the illusion of choice is the devaluation of relationships. In a world where matches are just another profile away, people may struggle to appreciate the value of a real connection. The ease of meeting new people online can create a disposable dating culture, where relationships are viewed as replaceable rather than something to be nurtured. When one small conflict arises, instead of working through it, individuals may choose to move on, believing that a "better" option is waiting for them. This approach makes it harder to build long-term emotional bonds, as people become accustomed to chasing short-term excitement rather than investing in deeper connections.

Additionally, dating apps and matchmaking platforms reinforce this illusion by using algorithms designed to keep users engaged. Many apps prioritize engagement over actual matches, ensuring that users stay active by presenting an ongoing stream of potential partners. Some platforms even withhold the best matches initially, keeping users searching longer in hopes of finding the "ideal" person. This creates a cycle where people feel they are always on the brink of meeting the perfect match, even if that match never truly materializes.

Despite these challenges, the illusion of choice can be overcome by shifting the mindset around dating. Instead of viewing online dating as an endless marketplace of options, individuals can focus on being intentional with their matches, investing time in getting to know people on a deeper level. Setting realistic expectations, prioritizing emotional connection over superficial traits, and recognizing that perfection is an illusion can help people navigate the digital dating world more effectively. Love is not about finding a flawless partner but about choosing to build something meaningful with someone who aligns with one's values and emotional needs. In the end, true connection comes not from having unlimited choices, but from the willingness to nurture the right one.

Beyond Surface-Level Attraction

In the digital dating era, where first impressions are often based on profile pictures and short bios, surface-level attraction plays a dominant role in determining initial interest. With dating apps encouraging quick decisions through swipes, people are more likely to judge potential partners based on appearance rather than deeper compatibility. While physical attraction is a natural and important part of romantic connections, lasting relationships require more than just good looks or a well-crafted profile. Moving beyond surface-level attraction means prioritizing emotional intelligence, shared values, and genuine compatibility over instant gratification.

One of the main challenges of digital dating is the emphasis on visual appeal. Studies have shown that people often make decisions about potential matches within seconds of viewing their profile picture, reinforcing the idea that looks play a crucial role in attraction. However, this approach can be misleading, as physical attraction alone does not guarantee emotional connection, compatibility, or long-term relationship success. Many people find that once they get to know someone, their level of attraction shifts based on personality, humor, emotional intelligence, and shared experiences. Conversely, an initial spark may fade quickly if deeper compatibility is lacking. True attraction develops through meaningful interactions, where qualities like kindness, ambition, empathy, and intellectual curiosity become more significant than physical features.

Another key factor in moving beyond surface-level attraction is the importance of emotional depth. While dating apps allow users to filter matches based on interests and preferences, they often fail to capture the essence of a person's character and emotional maturity. A well-written bio or a curated set of photos may showcase an individual's highlights, but it takes time and deeper conversations to understand their values, communication style, and emotional availability. People who focus solely on physical attraction may overlook partners who could be deeply compatible with them on a personal and emotional level. To build a meaningful relationship, individuals must engage in thoughtful conversations, ask deeper questions, and pay attention to how a person treats them and others.

Moreover, sustaining attraction requires more than just an initial spark. While chemistry may draw two people together, long-term relationships thrive on shared goals, mutual respect, and the ability to navigate life's challenges as a team. Couples who focus only on appearance or external qualities may struggle to maintain a strong bond when faced with real-world difficulties. On the other hand, relationships built on emotional connection and shared values tend to withstand the test of time, as both partners invest in growth, communication, and mutual support. Recognizing this can help people shift their dating mindset from seeking perfection to cultivating deeper, more meaningful relationships.

Ultimately, while physical attraction can ignite a romantic connection, true love is built on emotional intimacy, compatibility, and shared experiences. Moving beyond surface-level attraction requires intentionality, patience, and a willingness to explore a person's depth beyond their appearance. By focusing on what truly matters in a relationship, individuals can form connections that are not only exciting but also fulfilling, resilient, and enduring. In the end, genuine attraction goes far beyond the surface—it is found in the way someone makes you feel, the values they uphold, and the bond you create together.

Can AI Really Find "The One"?

With the rise of artificial intelligence in matchmaking, dating platforms claim to offer a more precise and scientific approach to finding love. AI-powered algorithms analyze vast amounts of data, including personality traits, interests, behavioral patterns, and even communication styles, to predict compatibility and suggest potential partners. But despite AI's ability to process information far beyond human capability, the question remains: can AI truly find "The One," or is love still too complex and unpredictable to be reduced to an algorithm?

AI-based matchmaking relies on pattern recognition and predictive modeling to connect individuals who share similarities or complementary traits. Dating apps like Hinge, OkCupid, and eHarmony use sophisticated data analytics to determine compatibility, considering factors such as values, emotional intelligence, and lifestyle preferences. Machine learning further refines recommendations over time by analyzing user interactions—who you swipe right on, how long you spend on a profile, and even the words you use in conversations. These AI-driven insights aim to remove the guesswork from dating by offering matches that align with long-term relationship success rather than just short-term attraction.

While AI can improve the efficiency of dating by filtering out less compatible options, it cannot fully predict or manufacture genuine chemistry. Love is influenced by subtle, intangible factors such as physical attraction, emotional connection, and shared experiences — elements that no algorithm can perfectly quantify. Even when AI finds two people who seem like an ideal match on paper, real-life interactions may not generate the expected spark. Human emotions are fluid, and relationships involve growth, change, and unexpected challenges that AI cannot foresee. The unpredictability of love means that even the best algorithm cannot guarantee that two people will truly connect or remain together in the long run.

Another limitation of AI matchmaking is that it relies heavily on user-provided data, which may not always be accurate. People often curate their online dating profiles to highlight their best qualities, sometimes exaggerating or misrepresenting certain aspects of their lives. If the data input into an algorithm is flawed or incomplete, the AI's matchmaking suggestions will also be compromised. Additionally, AI systems tend to reinforce patterns based on past behavior, which may unintentionally limit dating choices rather than encourage individuals to explore different types of connections that could lead to unexpected but meaningful relationships.

Despite these limitations, AI-driven matchmaking has led to many successful relationships, showing that technology can play a valuable role in helping people find love. By narrowing down the search and suggesting matches based on deeper compatibility rather than just looks, AI offers a more structured approach to dating. However, the final decision still rests with individuals — their willingness to invest time and effort into building a relationship, their ability to communicate effectively, and their emotional readiness for love.

Ultimately, while AI can assist in identifying potential partners, finding "The One" is still a deeply human experience. Love is not just about matching data points; it is about shared moments, emotional connections, and personal growth. AI may guide people toward compatible partners, but true love is built on authenticity, effort, and a touch of fate—something no algorithm can fully replicate.

Chapter 15
Virtual Heartbeats

In an age where digital interactions have become the foundation of many relationships, the concept of "virtual heartbeats" symbolizes the deep emotional connections formed through technology. Whether through long-distance relationships sustained by video calls, AI-driven companionship, or immersive virtual reality experiences, love and intimacy are no longer confined to physical presence. The way people connect, express affection, and build relationships has evolved, proving that emotions can transcend screens and digital interfaces. Virtual heartbeats represent the new rhythm of modern love—one that pulses through pixels, data streams, and shared online moments.

As technology bridges geographical distances and facilitates deeper emotional bonds, it also raises questions about the nature of intimacy and authenticity in digital relationships. Can virtual interactions truly replace physical touch, shared experiences, and the chemistry of in-person meetings? While some argue that digital love lacks the depth of real-world relationships, others find that meaningful emotional connections can flourish through consistent online communication, shared digital experiences, and even AI-generated companionship. The increasing role of artificial intelligence and virtual reality in relationships challenges traditional notions of love, intimacy, and human connection.

This chapter explores the rise of virtual heartbeats in modern relationships, examining how technology has redefined love, communication, and emotional closeness. It delves into the ways digital tools enhance relationships, the challenges of maintaining intimacy in virtual spaces, and the future of love in a world where virtual connections continue to grow. While technology may change the way people experience love, the core desire for connection remains the same—proving that, whether in person or through a screen, the heart still beats for love.

Digital Love and Emotional Intimacy

In the modern era, love is no longer confined to physical spaces or face-to-face interactions. The rise of technology has introduced new ways for people to form deep emotional connections, even when separated by vast distances. Digital love, facilitated by instant messaging, video calls, social media, and virtual reality, has reshaped the way individuals experience emotional intimacy. While some argue that technology has diluted the authenticity of relationships, others believe that digital connections can be just as meaningful, proving that love is not limited by physical presence but rather by the depth of emotional engagement.

One of the most profound aspects of digital love is the ability to maintain intimacy despite physical separation. Long-distance relationships, once difficult to sustain, now thrive through constant connectivity. Couples can share their lives through real-time video chats, voice messages, and social media updates, making them feel close even when miles apart. The immediacy of digital communication allows partners to express love, support, and vulnerability without the limitations of geography. This constant accessibility strengthens emotional bonds and fosters a deep sense of closeness, proving that relationships can flourish in digital spaces.

However, digital intimacy comes with unique challenges. Text-based communication lacks the non-verbal cues of in-person interactions, such as body language, eye contact, and touch, which are essential for building deep emotional connections. Misinterpretations can arise when messages are read without the intended tone, leading to misunderstandings that might not occur in face-to-face conversations. Additionally, the illusion of closeness created by frequent messaging can sometimes mask a lack of true emotional depth. Relationships built primarily on digital communication require conscious effort to ensure they are based on genuine connection rather than just the convenience of online interactions.

The role of AI and virtual reality in digital love further complicates the definition of emotional intimacy. AI-driven chatbots and virtual companions are increasingly being used to provide companionship, emotional support, and even romantic experiences. These technologies can simulate deep conversations, offer personalized interactions, and create a sense of emotional validation. Virtual reality takes digital love even further, allowing couples to engage in shared experiences, such as virtual dates or immersive environments where they can "be together" despite physical distance. While these advancements enhance digital relationships, they also raise ethical and psychological questions about whether AI-driven intimacy can truly replace human connection.

Ultimately, digital love and emotional intimacy depend on intentionality and authenticity. Technology can bridge gaps and enhance relationships, but real emotional connection requires trust, effort, and mutual understanding. Whether through daily video calls, handwritten digital letters, or deep conversations, maintaining intimacy in a digital relationship demands a commitment to emotional presence. While digital love may lack the physicality of traditional relationships, it proves that love is adaptable, resilient, and capable of thriving in any medium. As technology continues to evolve, so too will the ways people experience love, reminding us that true intimacy is not defined by physical space but by the depth of emotional connection.

The Role of VR in Modern Romance

Virtual reality (VR) is redefining the way people experience relationships, offering new ways to connect, interact, and build intimacy in the digital world. What was once considered science fiction is now becoming an everyday reality, as couples use VR to bridge distances, go on virtual dates, and even engage in fully immersive romantic experiences. As technology continues to advance, VR is poised to play an even greater role in modern romance, transforming not only long-distance relationships but also the very nature of dating, intimacy, and emotional connection.

One of the most significant ways VR enhances modern romance is by bridging physical distance in relationships. Long-distance couples, who once had to rely solely on text messages, phone calls, and video chats, can now interact in a shared virtual space, allowing them to "be together" despite being miles apart. VR platforms enable couples to hold hands, dance, watch movies, and visit simulated locations, creating the illusion of presence. This level of interactivity helps sustain emotional closeness, making long-distance relationships more immersive and fulfilling. Instead of just hearing a partner's voice or seeing them on a screen, VR allows couples to feel as if they are truly sharing experiences, strengthening their emotional bond.

Beyond long-distance relationships, VR is also transforming the dating experience by offering a new way for people to meet and interact. Virtual reality dating platforms allow users to create avatars and engage in social experiences without the pressures of traditional dating. Instead of swiping through profiles, people can meet in virtual environments that replicate real-world dating scenarios—like attending a concert, exploring a museum, or having dinner at a romantic restaurant. These immersive experiences help build emotional connections before transitioning to real-life meetings, allowing individuals to interact in a more natural and engaging way. This can be particularly beneficial for those who struggle with social anxiety or want to prioritize emotional compatibility over physical attraction.

VR also introduces new possibilities for intimacy and emotional expression. Advances in haptic technology, which simulates the sensation of touch, enable couples to experience physical interactions in a virtual space. This innovation allows for hand-holding, hugging, and even virtual kisses, adding a new dimension to digital intimacy. Some couples use VR to roleplay and explore shared fantasies, deepening their connection in ways that traditional digital communication cannot replicate. While these experiences cannot fully replace physical touch, they offer an alternative for couples separated by distance or individuals who seek intimacy in a virtual environment.

Despite its advantages, VR romance also presents challenges and ethical considerations. Some critics argue that virtual interactions may create a false sense of emotional intimacy, where people become more invested in the digital version of their partner than in the real person. There is also the concern that VR relationships might reduce the incentive for real-life interactions, leading to emotional detachment from the physical world. Additionally, as AI-driven virtual companions become more advanced, questions arise about whether people will form attachments to digital entities rather than pursuing human relationships.

Ultimately, the role of VR in modern romance is still evolving, but its impact is undeniable. By enhancing emotional connections, redefining dating experiences, and offering new ways to sustain intimacy, VR is revolutionizing the way people experience love. While it cannot replace the complexities of real-world relationships, it provides an innovative and immersive tool for deepening romantic bonds, proving that love can transcend not just distance but also the boundaries of reality itself.

How Technology Reinvents Long-Distance Love

Long-distance relationships (LDRs) have always been challenging, requiring patience, trust, and strong communication to thrive. In the past, couples relied on handwritten letters, landline calls, and the occasional in-person visit to maintain their connection. However, technology has completely transformed the way long-distance love is experienced, making it easier than ever for partners to stay emotionally connected despite being miles apart. With video calls, instant messaging, virtual reality, and AI-driven companionship, modern couples can share their lives in real-time, bridging the gap between physical distance and emotional closeness.

One of the most significant ways technology has reinvented long-distance love is through real-time communication tools. Video calling platforms like Zoom, FaceTime, and WhatsApp allow couples to see and hear each other at any time, making long-distance relationships feel less isolating. Unlike letters or phone calls of the past, video calls enable couples to share everyday moments—having dinner together, watching TV, or simply talking before bed—creating a sense of presence despite the physical separation. Messaging apps with voice notes, GIFs, and reactions further enhance communication, allowing for spontaneous interactions that mimic real-life conversations. These tools help maintain intimacy by making partners feel more involved in each other's daily lives.

Beyond communication, virtual reality (VR) is taking long-distance relationships to a new level by providing immersive experiences that make couples feel as though they are physically together. VR platforms allow partners to meet in digital spaces, whether it's taking a walk in a virtual park, exploring a fantasy world, or attending a live concert together. Advances in haptic technology, which simulates touch, even enable couples to hold hands, hug, or share a dance in the virtual realm. This level of interactivity strengthens emotional bonds and reduces the feeling of loneliness that often accompanies long-distance relationships. While VR cannot replace real-world intimacy, it offers an exciting alternative for couples who are separated by distance but want to share meaningful experiences.

Another groundbreaking advancement in long-distance love is AI-driven companionship and relationship-enhancing apps. AI-powered chatbots and virtual assistants can help couples maintain emotional closeness by sending reminders for special dates, offering personalized conversation prompts, and even analyzing communication patterns to suggest ways to strengthen the relationship. Additionally, couples' apps like Between and Love Nudge allow partners to track their relationship goals, share private messages, and send thoughtful gestures, such as digital love notes or surprise gifts. These tools help couples stay connected on a deeper level, ensuring that emotional intimacy remains strong despite the distance.

While technology has revolutionized long-distance love, it also presents challenges and potential pitfalls. Over-reliance on digital interactions can sometimes create a false sense of closeness, where couples feel emotionally connected online but struggle with real-life chemistry when they reunite. Additionally, constant access to each other through technology can lead to unrealistic expectations for instant replies and continuous availability, which can create pressure in the relationship. Maintaining a healthy balance between digital and real-life connection remains crucial for ensuring that technology enhances, rather than replaces, emotional intimacy.

Ultimately, technology has reinvented long-distance love by making it more interactive, immersive, and emotionally fulfilling. While physical presence will always be important in relationships, digital tools now allow couples to share their lives in ways that were once impossible. By leveraging technology mindfully, couples can not only sustain their love across distances but also strengthen their bond, proving that love is not defined by proximity but by the effort and commitment invested in keeping the connection alive.

Conclusion

As we navigate the complexities of love in the modern era, it is clear that technology has fundamentally reshaped the way people meet, communicate, and build relationships. From dating apps and AI-driven matchmaking to virtual reality experiences and long-distance digital intimacy, romance has entered an age where algorithms, data, and digital tools play a significant role in shaping human connection. While these advancements have expanded opportunities for love, they have also introduced new challenges, raising questions about authenticity, emotional depth, and the impact of technology on genuine relationships. However, one truth remains unchanged—love, in all its forms, continues to be one of the most powerful and enduring aspects of human life.

Throughout this book, we have explored how technology facilitates connections, from the instant gratification of swiping to the promise of AI-powered compatibility. While digital platforms can help people find potential partners, they cannot manufacture real chemistry, trust, or emotional resilience. True love is not about perfect algorithms or endless choices; it is about the willingness to commit, communicate, and grow with another person. The illusion of infinite options in the digital dating world often leads to decision fatigue, but those who approach relationships with intention and emotional depth are more likely to find meaningful connections. Love in the digital age is not just about who we match with—it is about how we nurture those relationships beyond the screen.

The evolution of technology in romance also highlights the importance of balance. While virtual spaces allow long-distance couples to stay emotionally connected, and AI companionship offers new forms of intimacy, human relationships are still rooted in experiences that go beyond digital interaction. The essence of love remains in the moments we share, the emotions we express, and the vulnerability we allow ourselves to feel. No matter how advanced technology becomes, it cannot replace the depth of a heartfelt conversation, the warmth of physical presence, or the unpredictability of falling in love.

As we move forward into an era where artificial intelligence, virtual reality, and digital dating will continue to evolve, it is crucial to remember that technology should serve as a tool to enhance relationships, not replace them. The future of love lies in our ability to adapt while preserving the core values of connection—trust, communication, and emotional authenticity. Whether we meet through an app, fall in love across different time zones, or explore relationships through digital avatars, the foundation of love remains the same: it is a choice, an effort, and an ongoing journey.

Love has survived centuries of change, from arranged marriages to letters carried across oceans, from telephone calls to instant messages, and now, from AI-driven matches to virtual reality interactions. Despite these shifts, the heart's desire remains unchanged—to find someone who understands, accepts, and walks alongside us through life. The digital age has provided new ways to experience love, but its essence remains timeless. No matter how technology evolves, love will always find a way to thrive—because, in the end, love is not just about connections made by algorithms, but about the moments, emotions, and choices that make those connections meaningful.